German East Africa, shewing Sphere of Opera[tions]

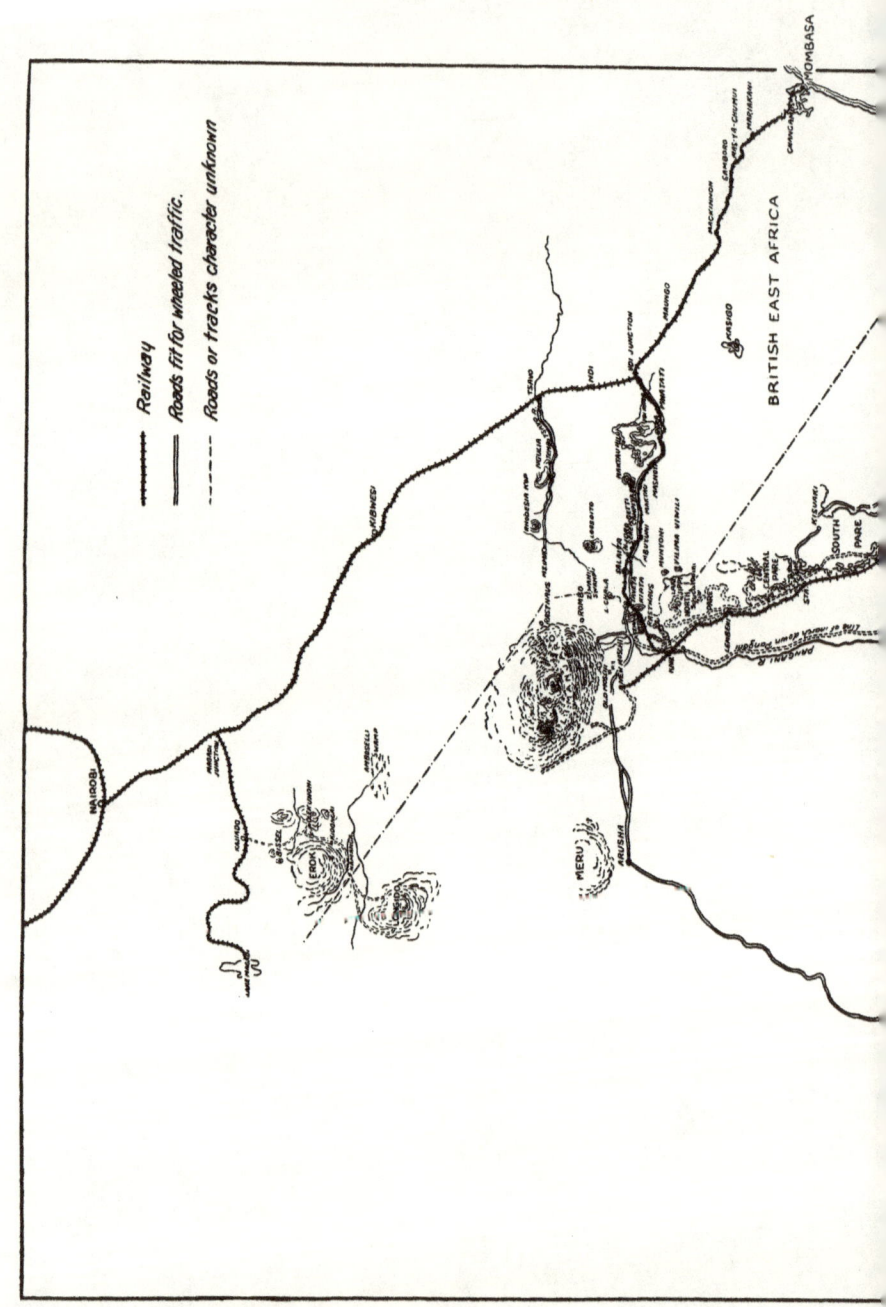

Gen. Smuts from Nairobi to the Rufigi River.

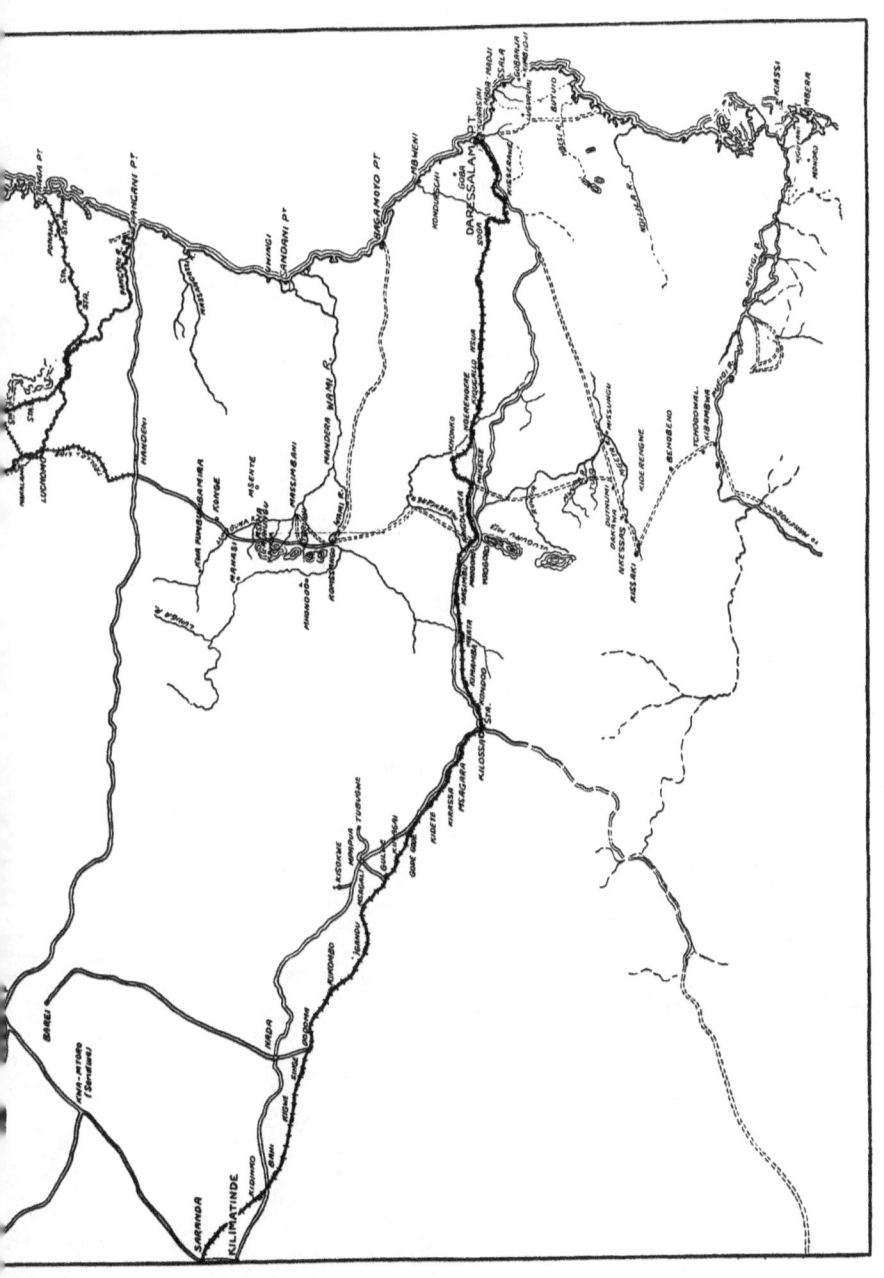

THE
2ND RHODESIA REGIMENT IN EAST AFRICA

LIEUT-COL A. E. CAPELL

FOREWORD BY
MAJOR-GENERAL SIR ALFRED H. M. EDWARDS,
K.B.E., C.B., M.V.O.
COMMANDANT-GENEREAL, RHODESIAN FORCES

The Naval & Military Press Ltd

Reproduced by kind permission of the Central Library,
Royal Military Academy, Sandhurst

Published by
The Naval & Military Press Ltd
Unit 10, Ridgewood Industrial Park,
Uckfield, East Sussex,
TN22 5QE England
Tel: +44 (0) 1825 749494
Fax: +44 (0) 1825 765701
www.naval-military-press.com
www.military-genealogy.com

© The Naval & Military Press Ltd 2008

In reprinting in facsimile from the original, any imperfections are inevitably reproduced and the quality may fall short of modern type and cartographic standards.

FOREWORD.

By Major-General SIR ALFRED H. M. EDWARDS, K.B.E., C.B., M.V.O., Commandant-General, Rhodesian Forces.

COLONEL CAPELL has asked me to write a foreword to his journal, which he has decided to call "The 2nd Rhodesia Regiment in East Africa"; the only thing that makes me somewhat diffident in accepting his invitation is that I doubt my ability to do justice to the subject.

As the ancient history of Rhodesia is to a large extent shrouded in the mystery of ages, and that of the middle distance, *i.e.* since the year 1890, has still to be published, it is more than pleasant to find someone who is determined that such a state of neglect and ignorance must not be allowed to continue, and that the children of Rhodesia of the present time and in years to come can have no excuse, as they have at present, for knowing little or nothing of the past and the doughty deeds of their forebears.

Having been present at the birth and, I regret to say, also the death of his Regiment—the 2nd Rhodesia Regiment—and acted to the best of my ability in *loco parentis* in Rhodesia while it was absent on Active Service in East Africa, I may perhaps be pardoned if I write feelingly about it.

Born strong and healthy, in its childhood it left Rhodesia for German East Africa, full of confidence and hope. Plunged without delay into an unhealthy area, it soon came in contact with its worst enemy—malaria—which before the end of the campaign sapped it of its strength and energy. This disease, however, never affected its heart, which remained sound and as strong as ever.

I think it may be acknowledged that the "*esprit de Rhodesia,*" which existed in the Regiment in a marked degree, invariably supported the effort of its members in their individual determination that no one should ever be in a position to say they had failed as soldiers to do their duty.

In the first stages of the Great War little or no notice was taken of what was happening in East Africa; thoughts were concentrated on our Western Front in Europe. In the middle phases, the advent in large numbers of troops from the Union of South Africa, with the complete change of command and plan of campaign, tended to put those troops in the background who for the previous year had borne the heat and burden of the day in that pestilential theatre of war, and it is to be regretted official records published so far throw little light on the inner history of the Campaign.

For this reason, if for no other, the value of a journal, which like this one gives the reader a very clear insight into what really did happen, and enables him to appreciate in some small degree the difficulties that had to be met and contended with, cannot be exaggerated.

Joining in General Smuts's offensive, the details of which have been more extensively chronicled, the Regiment more than kept up the good reputation it had already made for itself prior to that date. Its personality—if one may use the word—led others to appreciate its presence and moral support throughout this very trying period; and the gratitude of an India Regiment, the 130th Baluchis, clearly proved how great this was.

Of the occasions the Regiment was in action, Colonel Capell has written very clearly. The Regiment did what I always told them they would do, and that was, prove themselves worthy of the land they came from and the British race.

With General Smuts's departure the Regiment, reduced to a veritable skeleton, was placed on the Lines of Communication in the Central—Dar-es-Salaam—Ugige line of rail; and it was from here that they were ordered to return to Rhodesia, where the Head Quarters and emaciated remnants, numbering some 265 all ranks out of a paper strength of close on 800, arrived in March, 1917.

The Appendix shows an almost incredible record of the havoc played by disease during the Regiment's absence from

Rhodesia, and Colonel Capell's concluding pages help to explain how it was the Regiment's identity disappeared. On that subject I will not enlarge at length, but would like to explain that the real reason was that very few of those who served in East Africa were physically fit to proceed to Europe; and recruits at that stage were coming in in such very small numbers, far below the 20 per cent. a month required to replace casualties, that it was quite impossible for me, when I was asked to do so, to guarantee the regular supply of reinforcements asked for, if the Regiment was to be permitted to continue as a Rhodesian unit in the European theatre of war.

We in Rhodesia are very proud of what our men did during the Great War, and I have no hesitation in saying that we are prouder still of the 2nd Rhodesia Regiment—the only one that continued to serve until it could serve no longer—for the way it maintained in unknown hardships the traditions of our race and did credit to the land it came from.

In conclusion, I would like to congratulate the Author in his efforts, and to express the hope that the publication of his journal may prove the great success which it deserves.

Signed ALFRED H. M. EDWARDS,
Commandant-General,
Rhodesian Forces.

March 31st, 1922.

PREFACE.

LEST WE FORGET. RHODESIA 1914–1918.

THIS book does not purport to be a history of the East African campaign, which, compared with the great fields of operations in Europe, might be classed as a " small war."

Great events crowd so hard upon one another, the map changes day by day, lesser entities are becoming lost and swallowed up in greater formations, that there is a danger of the spirit of past noble deeds, great service and willing sacrifice being lost in oblivion and forgotten.

Where the Author appears to criticise military operations, he is simply recording impressions gathered by an individual, from careful study and observation of that portion of a " situation " coming directly under his notice.

Rhodesia did much more in service and sacrifice than is related in this small book, in which the Author has written only of the northern sphere of the theatre of war in East Africa, where the 2nd Rhodesia Regiment served. Another and a greater book might be required to tell the tales of the Southern Rhodesia Column, the Rhodesia platoon of the King's Royal Rifles, and of those independent free-lances who marched straight to the sound of the cannon.

> After the battles are over,
>   And the war drums cease to beat,
> And no more is heard on the hillside
>   The sound of hurrying feet;
> Full many a noble action
>   That is done in the days of strife,
> By the soldier is half forgotten,
>   In the peaceful walks of life.
>
> —*Ella Wheeler Wilcox.*

The 2nd Rhodesia Regiment in East Africa.

CHAPTER I.

ON October 22nd, 1914, the legislative council of Southern Rhodesia passed a resolution with the object of raising a contingent of 500 infantry, to be placed at the disposal of the Imperial Government.

The acceptance of this offer by the Secretary of State was communicated to the Resident Commissioner in a telegram dated November 16th.

Enlistment for the 2nd Rhodesia Regiment started on November 21st, and Major J. E. Nicholls was appointed Camp-Commandant at Salisbury until, on November 24th, he relinquished the post to Major Rowan Cashel, of the B.S.A.P., himself becoming Staff Officer for recruiting and Reserves. By this date the nucleus of a regiment was already in training, consisting of Lieut. A. Tribe, Acting-Adjutant and Musketry Instructor, Lieut. H. O. Coker, S.R.V. (E.D.), Sergt.-Major Smith, S.R.V. (E.D.), Sergt. Usher, Corpls. Blagrove and Hare (B.S.A.P.), and 93 N.C.O.'s and men.

On November 28th, " E " Coy, which had been embodied at Gwelo, arrived at Salisbury under the command of Capt. Allwyn Moses and Lieut. A. J. Dunn, and mustering 104 rank and file, commenced strenuous training daily at 5.45 a.m. and continued till 5 p.m.

Machine-gun and signalling instruction was undertaken by Lieut. Tribe and Sergt. Campbell respectively. On December 9th all ranks were inoculated against enteric, and made much of two days' holiday in consequence.

As Christmas approached people began to express their appreciation of their newly-formed regiment; the Mayor of Salisbury sent £27 10s., half a Koodoo bull was given by another, and Mrs. Hyde, of the Avenue Hotel, undertook to dine the rank and file of the Regiment at 5s. per head, the charge to include claret and hock cup and two whiskies and sodas. Of course it could not pay in kind, but without doubt the patriotic lady was repaid in full all the same.

On December 24th, the Regiment found a guard of honour for Rhodesia's new Administrator, Mr. Drummond Chaplin, on his arrival at the capital of the territory, but it was a sad day for the Regiment, for Capt. Allwyn Moses died at 11.35 a.m., and was buried that evening. He was an officer who could ill be spared, a keen and energetic soldier.

Christmas dinner at the Avenue Hotel was often recalled by the men in the lean years that followed. It was attended by the Commandant-General (Col. A. H. M. Edwards, C.B., M.V.O.), the Bishop of Southern Rhodesia, Major Murray, and Major Masterman.

On January 1st, 1915, Major A. E. Capell, D.S.O., was appointed to command.

Thus far, have I essayed to write in the third person, extracting items from a diary well kept by that gallant soldier, Major Cashel; but when I scan my effort it is dry as dust, so, in order to avoid the literary pitfalls into which all but the practised and trained tale-tellers and novelists must assuredly fall, if they try to put themselves in others' places—now to the first person singular (and plural).

I must cull from a difficultly-kept diary such little things as may reflect the light and life of those who entered the ranks of the 2nd Rhodesia Regiment. I found in camp every description of man: the pale young clerk, who yesterday sat at an office desk and nodded over a typewriter; the farmer, who left his growing crops to the mercies of a boss-boy; the prospector, who abandoned Golconda; the merchant, who shook his Fortunatus purse (and the impecunious, who had no purse to shake); the Government official, scarce rid of bureaucracy and red tape; the lawless, who brooked no' yoke; the sunburned Nimrod from the borderland, keen of eye and quick of ear; the youth in his teens, swearing with uplifted hand that he was twenty-five last birthday; the hard case, and the greenhorn; all were cheerfully submitting themselves to the heel of a military discipline, and a grinding, exacting routine: and what for? and why? Well, just because England called, not articulately, but in a low whisper that vibrated over an Empire, a fervent and trustful " S. O. S."

No thought of gain, recompense, remuneration—for they joined at Imperial rates, " the noble sum of thirteen-pence a day."

Camp and training irked indeed, for all were eager to march to *some*, to *any* seat of war, yet church parade was held on Sundays and the " dear old Bish " (The Lord Bishop of Southern Rhodesia)—no one seemed to know his surname—said again and again that it was a righteous war, with a big " R." Orderly room was held daily, and men told off for soldiers' "crimes," some blankly bewildered that such little things in civil life should assume such amazing proportions under the "King's Regulations" (a hard master, the King).

Sergt. Usher, B.S.A.P., was appointed Regt.-Sergt.-Major; Sergt.-Major Smith took on the role of Signalling Officer; Lieut. A. J. Dunn bloomed into an Adjutant and adopted long spurs and a faraway look; Tribe doted affectionately over a few machine-guns and a detachment of men I allowed him to pick from the Regiment.

Mr. O. H. Ogilvie, 6ft. 3in., broad, and with a swagger, marched on to parade.

The Commandant-General attended a battalion parade or two, and damned them with faint praise, as any real good general should.

A field day happened, when the Regiment held Hartman Hill—regiments are always holding Hartman Hill—and were attacked by the B.S.A.P. and the S.R.V. Result: very few S.R.V. and B.A.S.P. lived to tell the tale of carnage, and the General was just as usual impartially complimentary to all concerned: " just a h—l of a mess, I tell you "; but he taught us things, notwithstanding, and sometimes I thought he liked us, almost loved us, as his child.

Blagrove took on "Scouts"; another picked band, who followed strange spoor hither and thither, camouflaged their comings and goings, and were excused fatigues.

Mr. Gordon (ex-Captain, Scottish Horse), reported for duty as a company commander; he came with a South African War record, a liver, and a straight look in his eye. Then, on a certain Saturday (January 23rd, 1915), marched into camp from Bulawayo, Capt. Jesser-Coope with "C" and "D" companies, 138 rank and file and Lieut. Stokes. The Capt. did not take command of the Regiment, but he very nearly did. His canary-coloured tunic was impressive, to say the least; but best of all was the cheerful plucky smile that racking pain endured through long illness in pestilential country ever failed to banish.

Twenty-four points to nil was the score in favour of the Rhodesian Regiment when they played Salisbury Town on January 23rd at Rugger football.

So the time dragged on, and groups of men, as I passed hither and thither, chanted "Oh, when are we going away? Oh, when are we going away?"—and I could frame no answer, for shipping along the coast was dislocated and intercepted. Heavy rain began to fall, and water filtered through the crowded tents—tents so old that they may have sheltered some of these same old soldiers when they served in the Mashonaland rebellion of 1896. The camp was a quagmire, and a move to town billets was contemplated, in fact arranged against the wishes of all ranks, who scorned to seek shelter from less than active service hardships; it did not eventuate, and our faces were saved.

We dug trenches to drain the camp: trenches tactical, trenches strategical, trenches that were filled with wet and sloppy dummy figures for yelling troops to prod with bayonets. That the style of bayonet-fighting practised dated back to the Crimea did not seem to matter particularly. To jab something, and jab it hard, satisfied the primitive instinct and kept men hard and fit.

A deluge prevented our Footer match against the B.S.A.P. resulting in a famous victory. It was spoiled when the score stood at one goal in favour of the 2nd Rhodesia Regiment.

On February 21st all ranks were recalled from leave; the Regiment was to embark within a week. What glad tidings those were, what rejoicings and thrills they brought into existence —the corps would get away and the Empire might yet be saved!!!

Yet there was still one more opportunity to show our prowess in mimic warfare, and on February 24th we were ordered to attack the Transport Camp, held in strength by the B.S.A.P. We did that; but as the General ruled that "the whole thing was an absolute fiasco and a waste of an afternoon," we——dear, dear——.

Our military ardour damped in more ways than one, we adjourned to the Grand Theatre, where the regimental exponents of the gentle art of fisticuffs stood up and battered each other before a very appreciative assembly.

I find I have failed to enter Orders that apparently were issued on February 21st, 1915. They do not stand in the regimental books, but may be usefully recorded here for the gain and benefit of young soldiers. The perpetrator was undiscovered, or protected by his comrades.

    SENTRIES ORDERS. 2ND RHODESIA REGIMENT.
    The extent and the front of his " beat " he must ken,
    And take charge of all Government property then:
    That is, all such property exposed to his view,
    And take charge of his post as a soldier should do.
    He must turn out the Guard at all times of the day
    To the Administrator, and make no delay;
    To the O.C. in uniform, once this is due,
    The Orderly Officer and armed parties too,
    Grand Rounds, Reveille, Retreat and Tattoo.

In a soldierly manner he'll traverse his beat,
At each limit turn outwards look promptly and neat;
When halted, will turn to his front and to please
In a manner that's military stand at his ease.
He saluteth all officers, 'cording to rank,
Whether posing in mufti or military swank;
To those under Field Officer pause in his strut
And bring his hand smartly to small of the butt.
To Field ditto and those of superior position
Will present arms at once or regret the omission.
He will not leave his post unless he's commanded
By Non.-Com. in charge, or he'll be reprimanded.
He'll observe special orders whenever he's told,
And stop vehicles entering camp from the road.
At the " Slope " to his front he'll salute all armed forces,
Nor talk to a soul, nor lounge in his courses.
'Tween Tattoo and Reveille he'll shout out like Hell.
" Halt, who comes there ? " and " Pass, friend, all's well."

SPECIAL ORDERS.

All special orders must be strictly obeyed,
And tact must be used when approaching a maid:
Blow her a kiss, don't USHER her in,
And compare her to Venus, though ugly as sin.

Salisbury, February 21st, 1915.

The allotted time is flying, and on February 25th, His Honour the Administrator (Mr. Drummond Chaplin) inspected and addressed the Regiment in farewell terms, in the presence of a proud and appreciative audience of townsfolk, parents, relations and sweethearts. The regimental bosom swelled with pride, emotion, and martial ardour. Can it be wondered at, that an " after-the-ball " sort of feeling crept in and pervaded it ?—on receipt of a wire on the morning of the 26th to the effect that the ship was detained at Durban discharging cargo, and would not be available until March 5th or 6th. On Tuesday, March 2nd, a farewell church service was held in the Cathedral, and on the 3rd a farewell concert was held in camp, and a farewell address given by His Worship the Mayor of Salisbury. Oh, Lord ! For farewell ! !

On the 4th an inter-company go-as-you-please run of four miles to Ladley's Huts was held in a deluge of rain. An excellent corrective. " C " Company was a good winner; " B " did well; " A " and " D " followed in the order named.

At-long-last the day of departure (March 6th, 1915) arrived, and the " Regiment in the making," became a " Regiment in being." It rained—it always did rain when we did anything.

Horses were entrained for Beira, and Major Masterman, Embarkation Officer, and Capt. McQueen, Transport Officer, went with them.

The Commandant-General said good-bye, read a farewell message from the High Commissioner, and another from the Board of Directors of the British South Africa Company.

Sunday, 7th. No! not gone yet!

But Monday saw entraining commencing at 6 a.m., and the first train left the camp siding at 6.45. From thence to Salisbury railway-station, where it remained ten minutes; the second train followed at half-an-hour's interval under the command of Major Cashel.

Crowds of friends, relations and well-wishers saw the Regiment leave, and those left behind on the platform seemed sadder than those in the crowded train; the tension of suspense had been long-drawn; the atmosphere was electrical and charged with feeling. Only a great mental effort brought those brave bright smiles to the tear-charged eyes of wives, mothers, sisters, sweethearts; and what it cost them to wave those white handkerchiefs, God and the angels only know.

Umtali town turned out in strength to see us pass through; the Mayor gave us an address and a purse of £25; the C.O., the diary says, " responded in a few well-chosen words." The train was loaded with smokes, good wishes, and no little beer, as Umtali wished us " God-speed."

A few miles east of Umtali, when we crossed the border into Portuguese East Africa, we cast off childish things and became an entity. For months the Commandant-General had " stuffed and taught us and crammed " and damned and praised us whole-heartedly and impartially as a soldier should. Bishop Beaven had appealed to our spiritual fundamentals, exhorted us to be material and cold-blooded, and rubbed in the righteous war with the big " R " and the Red, White and Blue, until we didn't know whether he was parson or soldier. The Administrator had addressed us in terms measured and flawless, Mayors and Municipalities had slapped us on the back, men had drunk to us, women had wept for us, and between them they had forged and fashioned a Regiment—a Regiment conceived in the womb of war, born in an hour of stress, and nurtured on the breast of need, that had clambered to its stature and cast off swaddling clothes.

But how was it that Rhodesia could raise the Regiment?—that any able-bodied Rhodesian could leave his interests, his farm, his fortune and family in a land thickly peopled with savages?

Trenchant questions these !—and " lest we forget " let them be answered. Yes ! lest we forget that a handful of men, trained for war, ready and keen, fit for any front, any fight, remained behind to do their duty—a duty that hurt, as bitter as gall and wormwood, and to-day, because of them, Rhodesia can proudly boast that no colony or territory of the Empire sent so large a proportion of its manhood to answer the mute call of an anxious-eyed motherland in need of her sons.

This handful of men was collectively styled the B.S.A.P. Called out " on active service," they stand undecorated, for no medal comes their way; but an unstinted meed of honour is their due, for they permitted, sanctioned, and guaranteed the exodus, and fully redeemed an unspoken pledge. Cede ye to them the right of the line, as a tribute to worth, for value received.

CHAPTER II.

BY 10.20 a.m. on March 9th embarkation on board the s.s. *Umzumbi*, 5,000-ton Bullard King liner, was complete. The holds had been filled up with mattresses and tables; not much of quarters for a rough sea voyage, but good enough for active service. I called on the Governor, Major Pery de Lind, and invited him to the ship, and about 5.15 His Excellency came aboard with his Staff and his daughter. The Regiment fell in, a salute was sounded, and the genial Governor shook hands with the officers before being entertained in the smoking room; later, as his boat pulled shorewards, three hearty British cheers followed in its wake, and forged another link of friendship with an old and staunch ally. At 5.30 the propellers moved and the good ship started.

The morning of the 10th witnessed a fresh breeze blowing, a fair sea running, and human freight lying about the decks in all stages of sea-sickness—most unromantic of illnesses. Pass we this, till 7 o'clock on the morning of March 14th, we berthed alongside the *Cluny Castle* off Mombasa—Mombasa still asleep. At 10 a.m. a Major, quite unmistakably on the Staff, and not long out of India—two years later he was a wiser, but not, I think, a sadder man, and a close observer would have gathered he was a Staff Officer—stepped on board.

We learn here that there are not more than 10,000 troops in East Africa, that the only European troops are a battalion of the Loyal North Lancashire Regiment and a handful of East African Mounted Rifles. The time was tense and critical, it was hard on the heels of the regrettable disaster at Tanga and the reverse at Jasin, neither of which was calculated to improve *morale*. It struck us that the Regiment was more welcome in the country than people cared to show or own.

At 10 a.m. on the 15th disembarkation commenced—that is, if flinging kit-bags from the main deck into lighters below can be so-called; it was not a good plan, and as they had to be re-sorted on shore, work was duplicated and time wasted; some kits, of course, went overboard into the sea, but the moment required a joke of some sort. Col. Baily, the Base Commandant, ordered a parade, and welcomed the Regiment, and Ptes.

Strobel, Clark and Kelly went into hospital—I don't mean because of the welcome.

The troop train steamed out of Mombasa at 4 p.m., it having taken $5\frac{1}{2}$ hours to disembark and entrain, notwithstanding the men had worked splendidly. An accident on the line prevented the train getting past Changamwe, some four miles out of Mombasa ; so 1,000 bottles of beer were ordered from the B.E.A. Corporation—now don't exclaim, but just work it out—and an impromptu smoking concert was held under the great mango trees beside the line until 11 o'clock, when our westward journey was recommenced.

Let us establish a literary exception, and pass by the teeming herds of game on the shimmering plains and get to our destination, Kajiado, on the Magadi soda-lake line, the base for operations towards Longido Mountain, that little morsel of German territory that we claimed by right of conquest. Wind-swept, dirty, bleak, strewn with dumps of grain, bully-beef and stores, was the Kajiado we reached in the early hours of March 17th. By 7 a.m. the Staff-Officer, Capt. Nobel, was dug out ; he was in a somewhat uncertain mood, but kindly conducted us, with a take-it-or-leave-it sort of air, to our camping ground, where tentage had been provided. He told us there were three Colonels and 35 rank and file of Indian troops on the station ; and we realised that at-long-last we had joined the Army, and incidentally the Indian Expeditionary Force.

Dawn disclosed to us the distant base of Kilimanjaro, the upper features clouded in mystery and gossamer ; a sight to give pause to the most materialistically minded. She rose from a seeming plain abrupt, majestic, and asleep. Then, as we watched, of a moment she stirred, the veil was drawn aside, and her sweet pale face became suffused with rose-red blushes, as from the first morning kiss of the sun's warm lips : and she was awake. The fleeting colour faded, leaving a snow-white head and a body draped in blue-grey robes. Ah ! *there* was something to fight for, something to win ! To think that alien hands should hold her, the Queen of a wide domain, one of the fairest things of Africa. No ! she must be saved, to brood there for countless years over a fair land and a clean people, a people bearing a name as unsullied as her own pure and eternal snows, a heart as rich as her hidden gold, a tear as limpid as her own mountain streams, a frown as black as her blasted crags, and a smile as sweet as her sunny slopes. Vale ! Nature's Queen of Eastern Africa.

Col. Drew, commanding the Magadi district, requested

a parade of the Regiment on the 18th, in fatigue dress, without arms, and did not make a speech ; albeit he told me afterwards he very much liked the look of the men. Then, on the following day, welcome news came that the Germans were concentrating to attack Longido : two companies of the 2nd Rhodesian Regiment to be ready to re-inforce.

At 7.30 a.m. on March 20th, General J. Stewart, Indian Army, inspected the Regiment and just said : " I had expected to see a regiment that would require some training ; I will pay you the highest compliment by sending you to the front to-day." And true enough at 4.30 p.m. we were off to Namanga to relieve the Loyal North Lancs. and form general reserve for Longido.

Before leaving we were given fifteen horses and saddles of sorts, on which we mounted Blagrove's scouts for reconnaissance purposes.

At 8.15 p.m. we halted at Emelelo, but our transport being of a very poor order of ox-drawn wagons, did not arrive till 10.30, having accomplished ten miles in six hours. Rain started as reveille sounded at 2 a.m., and then the wagons stuck before getting a mile on the road ; so we breakfasted and waited for the roads to dry. Not a propitious start, but the men were cheery enough ; says one : " Well, how do you like soldiering ? " Answer : " A.1.—If I'd known what it was like, I should have begun long ago " ; he was drenched to the skin, and held in his hand a billy of coffee brewed from a puddle in the road.

Soon after mid-day we marched into Bissel, a precariously-situated camp, surrounded by hills within effective rifle range ; later on the fact was grasped that we were not engaged in an Indian " hill war." Capt. Gordon was holding this L.-of-C. post with 100 Indian troops.

A strange feature of the march were the telephone poles 30ft. high to prevent the numerous giraffes catching their necks in the wire, and with a thick thorn boma at the base lest the rhinoceros should rub against them.

By 4 p.m. on March 22nd the oxen had sufficiently recovered to attempt an eight-mile march to Olekunoni, another death-trap, into which a subaltern and 100 Indians had been thrown, but the Huns didn't know.

Another hill fortress, Kiddongai, was reached on the 24th ; here one-and-a-half companies of the Kapurtalas were offering themselves as a bloody sacrifice.

At 7 a.m. on the 25th a Regiment—very proficient in packing wagons and moving off silently in the dark—marched into Namanga, the post immediately in support of Longido, and about eleven miles distant from that mountain.

Tribe took over two machine-guns from the Loyal North Lancs at Lone Hill, a station in a salient in our line of communication, and about six miles from Namanga. We were now in possession of four Maxims, and a lot of pride in the detachment. The Regiment was cheerful in spite of a dirty, dusty camp, and in the anticipation of a scrap of some sort. Perhaps the main guard parading " for the stick " daily under such circumstances irked a bit, and possibly caused some grousing, but it became almost popular and a regimental honour from the day that a man of another regiment said to a smart sentry : " What are you doing ? *We* don't mount no ruddy main guards ! "

Here we met face to face that strange phenomenon—not peculiar to one, or any war, but common to all—the relaxation of discipline at the commencement of active service. It seems to be forgotten, not alone by rank and file, but by responsible officers, that war is the game of the Army, the battle the match, the discipline the training ; yet what football team would relax its training with a match in view ? No ! it like the Army should intensify its training, add rigidity to its discipline ; the footballer does it, although the Army doesn't, yet the principle is enunciated in military law by the stiffening up of sentences. Result, those battalions that inadvertently or purposely relax the bonds too far, are the cause of disaster to themselves and disaster to others, disaster to our arms too often encountered in the early stages of our wars ; or at best they are sent back to a rest-camp ostensibly to recuperate on Lines of Communication, in reality to reconstruct and train, train, train, in much anguish of spirit, with many close order parades, countless main guards, and generally " Hell," from which they emerge " fit for active service."

On Wednesday, March 31st, orders were issued for the withdrawal of troops from the Kajiado-Longido line ; the 2nd Rhodesian Regiment to form the rear-guard during the operation. So the Regiment took over all the pickets at Namanga from Indian details, and two companies—" C " and " D "—marched to Longido and relieved the Loyal North Lancs, who had there prepared tea and cooked rations, and waited on our fellows—after their arduous march—in splendid fashion. On April 1st a report that proved to be true came into camp, that a convoy escort of Indian troops, having handed over their charge between Kidongai and Olekunoni, were returning to the latter station when they were attacked by eight mounted Germans and fifteen Askari, who had apparently been tapping our telephone line. Two Indians were killed, two severely wounded, and the remainder captured. The bolts of their rifles were then removed, and with scant courtesy they were returned to our lines, a proceeding that smacked strongly of the Boer War. All available mounted men from Longido and Namanga were ordered out. Lieut. Graham took 25 Rhodesians, mounted on whatever he could find with four legs and capable of bearing a man's weight : a weird troop of cavalry. He stayed out two days in the vilest weather, but was too badly mounted to catch up with the raiders. The 17th Indian Cavalry and E.A.M.R. came back to dinner after a few hours futile search.

About this time Captain Ogilvie went into hospital with a badly poisoned arm, and our ranks generally were beginning to thin from sickness caused by exposure, fever, and above all by the sun overhead, for the Regiment had not yet got helmets, and the smasher hat of Rhodesia was as useful as tissue paper five degrees south of the African equator.

A night-alarm on April 5th. An Indian soldier—one of a convoy escort approaching Namanga—rushed into camp, and breathlessly reported the convoy heavily attacked. In a very few minutes Capt. Coker and 50 2nd Rhodesian Regiment were despatched to rescue the convoy from enemy hands, and within an hour he had brought it safely in. It was then reported that the firing had been at charging lions. A morning reconnaisance disclosed a cow full of lead and nickel !

British troops seldom for long let the football lie idle, and two soccer matches were arranged against the Loyal North Lancs. The first resulted in two goals to nil in our favour, and the second in a draw. It is only fair to admit that the Lancs had marched ten miles on the day they were beaten.

Much drudgery of active service attended the preparations for the general withdrawal : loading supply waggons, constant convoy work, picketing summits of mountains by day and by night, living on bad or scanty rations ; but all was borne with the indomitable spirit of cheerfulness, characteristic of Rhodesians in general and the Regiment in particular.

" C " and " D " companies marched in from Longido under Major Cashel at 10 a.m. on April 7th, and thus we relinquished the scrap of enemy territory gallantly assaulted and taken by the troops under Colonel Drew, Indian Army, in the early days of the conflict : our one tangible success. Should it ever have been taken ? Might it not have been kept ? Pregnant questions ! The first was asked and answered before our Regiment landed at Mombasa. The second can be answered in four monosyllables, " No, it could not ! " And why ? Because the enemy were daily strengthening ; because our only means of supply to Nairobi and Uganda was the one single line

of railway—300 miles of it between Nairobi and the coast—
passing through a forest-clad country lending itself to small
enterprises, possessing several large bridges, and vulnerable at
almost any point. Should any serious break in the line occur,
or an enemy force throw itself across it, disaster to our arms
must result. Our forces were small, and a large proportion
could not rightly be left to hold a sentimental line culminating
in a strategically useful mountain, that tactically could be retaken,
or cut off at any future time, given sufficient troops to prosecute
the campaign as a whole. It must be tacitly accepted that we
were acting on the defensive against an enemy numerically
stronger and superior in *morale* by reason of initial victories,
and it was clearly the duty of the G.O.C. to so strengthen the
defence that it would have the best possible chance of with-
holding his opponent until such time as the help, that England
never fails to send, arrived. Further, it must have been clear
to him that any serious attack on Kidongai or Olekunoni, posts
on the Line of Communication before referred to, would almost
certainly succeed, and in that event the troops at Namanga and
Longido would be cut off and " in the air."

At best the retention of Longido could only " contain "
hostile troops at Moshi, and as Moshi was many long marches
distant, and fed by a railway, the enemy would have little
cause for alarm. We were not even shaking a fist at him.

The withdrawal did not work without a hitch, as is usually
reported to be the case. The convoy started at 3 p.m. and got
to Kidongai, a distance of nine miles, at midnight. The road
was good, but the waggons, carrying only between three and
four thousand pounds, were overloaded, so poor were our cattle,
so inexperienced our drivers. On April 9th a belated start
was made at 8 a.m. and a halt of the troops called at 10.50 a.m.
at a point that the convoy reached at 12 noon, having
accomplished $2\frac{1}{2}$ miles in 4 hours. The oxen had had just one
hour's grazing in 21 hours, namely from 7 to 8 a.m., so
Capt. Sheen, the transport officer—the only man in the column
outside of the 2nd Rhodesian Regiment and E.A.M.R. who
knew an ox from a nilghai—on refusing to proceed under these
conditions was placed under arrest. That broke the axle, and
the machinery stopped altogether till Col. Drew came along,
took a broad common-sense view of the situation and released
him, and in accordance with his advice had the loads redis-
tributed, when it began to rumble again. By the periods the
oxen were kept under the yoke, it would appear to be a forced
march or hasty retreat, but it was in reality just a tardy procession.
By the time we reached Olekunoni the animals had had precisely

3½ hours grazing in 38 hours, and so it progressed until, on April 14th, the Regiment reached Kajiado, after a march conducted by those who were inexperienced for the most part, and unacquainted with the vagaries and vicissitudes of African transport. Had a 1901 Boer commando observed such a convoy, it would have collectively thanked the " Good God," and have been all over, round and behind it, in the turn of a wagon-wheel. The majority of our troops praised Allah on a successful issue.

Bissel was very rightly retained, as it could easily be reinforced from Kajiado and served as a protective post for Nairobi.

The Regiment went into camp at Kajiado as general reserve, with a promise that if any scrapping took place anywhere, it would be called upon.

Three men down with sunstroke! Ah! when will those helmets come? The climate is a stronger adversary than the Hun ; it takes a toll every day, blazingly and persistently.

CHAPTER III.

OUR stay at Kajiado was not prolonged as, on April 16th, urgent orders were received for one company to move to Tsavo, and three companies to Voi ; so as usual we packed up in a pouring rain, dropped " C " Company at Tsavo at 11.30 p.m., " A ", " B " and " D " arriving at Voi 2.30 a.m. on April 18th. Orders were at once received for two companies to return to Tsavo, so " A " and " D " were re-entrained, leaving only " B " Coy, at Voi, destined for Maktau. " A " and " D " arrived at Tsavo at 4.30 p.m. on April 18th, where orders were waiting for a company to march to Mzima. We were still unequipped with serviceable gear, boots being completely worn out, and men marching barefoot. I bought 200 yards of pugaree cloth to wrap round their silly smashers, and took the boots off the very feet of the Kashmir Rifles stationed at Tsavo. Thus, on the morning of the 19th, " C " Company under Capt. Jesser Coope was enabled to start out with 400 porters for Mzima. Col. Vickers, who had recently taken over the line of posts from Mzima to Tsavo, went with " C " Company, also Major Cashel.

Here, camped on the very ground where the man-eaters of Tsavo exacted such heavy toll from the bridge builders, the little events happened that mean so much to men on active service, yet seem so insignificant in times of prosy peace. Fever and dysentery hovered in the camp, and laid a hand on everyone ; none escaped, and many went to hospital. A mail—our first—came in from Rhodesia. Boots and helmets and new short rifles were issued, and tardily we became equipped. We learnt that " B " Company marched from Voi to Maktau on April 21st, and also of a little scrap at Mzima on the 24th. Capt. Ogilvie put in an application to resign on the 25th, or for sufficient leave to go to Umtali on " urgent private affairs." I reluctantly granted the latter, and we did not see him again. Blagrove took out his scouts on a three days unsuccessful hunt for the Huns, who blew up the line near Kibwesi, killed two natives and seven mules ; whereupon His Majesty's armoured train " Undaunted " gets very much upset, and barges round in a great state of ineffectual excitement.

16   THE 2ND RHODESIA REGIMENT

On April 29th I started out together with Hare and Major McClintock for Mzima, to visit " C " Company there, and found them camped in mud and filth, in little grass bandas run up in palm grove swamps. On the low hill 400 yards away was a well-constructed and strongly-entrenched earthwork, held by K.A.R. and Indian troops which was on the point of being abandoned in order to have all the troops under the concealment of the palm grove, which was ankle-deep in liquid mud, in which the crowded troops wallowed thickly. Fortunately the intention was not carried out. Much hard patrol work was being done, and frequent little skirmishes took place in the thick bush that covered the country like a mantle. It was a most unsavoury place, and officers and men were yellow with fever and dysentery.

With the abandonment of Longido a new military situation had been created, which it may be advisable to outline here: it was the assumption of a strong defensive attitude, protecting our communications between Mombasa and the interior, and I do not think anyone will be hardy enough to question the wisdom of adopting it at the moment.

A factor bearing on that situation, but not generally appreciated, was the disaffection of some of our own Indian troops. The extent of it might be guessed, but could not be gauged. Desertions to the enemy were not infrequent. German propaganda was undoubtedly responsible for this unsatisfactory state of affairs, for with their customary astuteness they appealed to the strong religious natures of their opponents, by fastening posters to trees in the vicinity of our camps, and scattering pamphlets at places where our patrols would be likely to pass; stating in Hindustani that the Kaiser was in Constantinople, the chief of Mohamedanism, and Emperor of India; inviting desertion and promising security.

A study of the map will reveal the Uganda railway running from Mombasa north-west to Nairobi, three hundred miles distant. Almost parallel with it and at a distance varying from 100 miles at Korogwe and 75 miles at Moshi, is the German Usambara railway from Tanga to Moshi. The country within the parallels—namely, until Voi is reached—is covered in dense thorn bush, and is waterless and practically unexplored, if one excepts the Umba river, distant some 80 miles from our railway: evidently this was not the danger point.

From Voi to Kibwesi, a distance of some 80 miles, the line ran through a thickly-bushed, well-watered country, and any portion of it within 80 miles of Moshi, the German railhead and headquarters, which was situated about the centre. This was obviously our weak spot, especially as it contained several important bridges and culverts. From Kibwesi to Nairobi the country is mostly open plain, and unfavourable for operations from the enemy's point of view. The Germans held a line of about 40 miles, with Rhombo on their left, Taveta with strong force thrown forward to Umbuyuni in the centre, and Lake Yipe on their right. To meet this situation the G.O.C., established two lines of posts : one from Tsavo to Mzima, a distance of 37 miles, with an intermediate station, Tembo, 20 miles distance from Tsavo ; Mzima was opposite Rhombo, and the enemy line of posts on the foothills of Kilimanjaro and distant about 18 miles. The other from Voi to Maktau, some 40 miles (8 miles of which could be traversed by a strategic railway under construction), with an intermediate post at Bura at 20 miles, and Mashoti 26 miles. At both Mzima and Maktau were stationed about 1,000 troops. At Kibwesi was a battalion.

Maktau was opposite to Taveta, with the enemy outpost at Mbuyuni 14 miles in front.

Mzima and Maktau—once established as strong entrenched positions at the termini of lines of posts, each able to furnish a mobile column of 300 rifles and complement of machine-guns—might be likened to the extreme cutting tips of the horns of a stag beetle : the smaller posts on the lines of communication to the serrated teeth. Should therefore the enemy send any considerable force towards our line of rail, before he had vanquished either Mzima and Maktau, he would be in grave danger of the horns closing in round him. Should he send small raiding parties, the commotion of explosion or incident must arouse the line of posts, and a gauntlet would have to be run to regain friendly terrain. Thus the system imposed hazardous adventures, if any, upon our opponents ; risks which small bodies occasionally took, but without effecting commensurate damage to our railways. Whether the plan devised by Gen. Sir Michael Tighe, the G.O.C., is open to criticism or not, it in every way fulfilled its purpose and intention until such time as reinforcements arrived and protection of rail communication became a minor factor in the situation.

That the enemy was not more enterprising on a larger scale about this period may possibly be attributed to the fact that he thought reinforcements had arrived ; for at the moment of our arrival in the country his attitude had been threatening. He would, however, have heard of the disembarkation of European troops, probably a very much exaggerated account from native sources ; and to such an extent, and so rapidly had we been moved, that he had seen them at Longido,

Kajiado, Voi, Maktau, and Mzima within a very short space of time, and might easily have been misled as to our strength. In point of fact, since the fight at Jassin, the Germans had displayed little more activity than we had, and had contented themselves with holding in strength a line of posts 40 miles in length along the foothills of Kilimanjaro from Lake Yipe to Rhombo, and roughly distant 15 miles from our defensive line. These intervening miles were neutral ground, or "No Man's Land," and actively patrolled by both contending sides; the country between Maktau and Taveta being for the most part open bush and extensive dambos, that round Mzima and Tsavo and towards Rhombo being so thickly covered with thorn bush that it was almost impenetrable, except along rhinoceros, elephant, or big game tracks. So dense was it that a patrol of some 200 rifles and some 60 porters on one occasion passed a German patrol of about the same strength at a distance less than 150 yards and yet neither was cognisant of the other's existence. Our suspicions were certainly aroused by a single rifle shot, but scouts sent in the direction of the sound failed to find anything, and it was not until the next day that another patrol found the Hun's spoor running parallel to ours and in the opposite direction. The bush swarmed with rhinoceros, that not infrequently charged and scattered our columns and bundled up and down the line of discarded porter loads, tossing them hither and thither. Single file was the only possible formation in this country, and a column of 200 rifles with complement of machine-guns and carriers would stretch out to a mile in length. Flank escorts or guards were out of the question, and the risk of attack had to be run and be compensated for by the hope of surprising an enemy.

It was obviously essential to either side to patrol diligently "No Man's Land" to learn what his opponent was doing or contemplating. Either side had strong posts, that should be reconnoitred and if possible attacked or harassed; and herein the Germans presented to us an object-lesson. Information by intelligence agents was of little avail; they could learn next to nothing in the bush that covered the country as a dark night. But the enemy posted in trees a few native scouts within rifle-shot hearing of each other, and of their posts; and a single shot would be fired and taken up and repeated by each in turn until the alarm reached the ear of the post commander. Then he would give practical evidence that he appreciated our own maxim "that the offensive is the soul of defence," for, without exception, within half an hour of the first shot ringing out, an attack in the bush would develop on our flank or rear, a indecisive action be fought, and the German strong post remain undiscovered. A decisive action could not be fought where fire effect could not be observed, and where shock action was precluded by reason of impenetrable bush. A charge was impossible; the German system of far-flung native observers posted in trees was a superior method to ours in gathering local information of enemy movement, and because of it, we were never able to locate their strong posts, as we were offered battle a mile or more from them. On the other hand, we in our positions were usually startled into the knowledge of the proximity of an enemy force by the crack of rifles and by bullets falling in our camps or picket posts. He carried out an active defensive by gaining early information of our movements and then attacking us in a situation and on ground chosen by himself, some miles in advance of his defensive post.

Conditions round and in front of Maktau were somewhat different, the country being more open. Patrols more often came in touch with one another, and the encounter was usually decisive, but generally speaking there was sufficient bush to afford cover from view, and to introduce the element of surprise, and the side executing the surprise usually heavily defeated the other. On the whole, honours in these patrol encounters during this phase of the campaign were about even.

CHAPTER IV.

SOME six miles north of Mzima stands an isolated hill in a sea of lava and bush. It commands a wide view in every direction over the surrounding country, and might have been useful as an observation post if it had been possible to see anything but thorn bush at twenty yards distance. Rhinoceros in numbers, elephant and countless herds of game roamed through it, but were seldom seen without arduous still hunting and stalking.

To spot troops moving through this country from "Signal Hill"—as this eminence was called—was an impossibility; and yet ten men were detailed daily at 6 a.m. precisely to march to that hill to observe; to march by the one-and-only road over those lava slabs, crevices and ragged chasms; through that rock-strewn gulch, narrow and treacherous; a deadly spot in which to entrap or surprise an enemy. Less than 100 men could not scout the surroundings of this solitary secluded pathway, yet ten victims were offered daily, offered as a sacrifice by inexperience.

The obvious happened on May 8th. Signal Hill was being held promiscuously by some thirty of the 130th Baluchis for the time being; the enemy made a demonstration towards them, and ambushed the daily patrol. The men had no chance in the narrow gulch; they fought where they stood, as the empty cartridge-cases testified, but Pte. Townsend, Signaller Wells, Ptes. Potts and Nelson died there, shot through and through, bayonetted, beaten to death with rifle-butts, and stripped of their clothing. Corpl. Faber was missing: it later transpired that he was wounded, but knowing a little of the German language had been placed on a stretcher and taken to the German camp at Rhombo, where he subsequently died of his wounds. And Bulawayo homes, from whence these men hailed, heard of "an affair of patrols," instead of the "affair of a fool."

Our ammunition at this time was most unreliable; many rounds had proved "misfires" and "blowbacks," when testing the rifles recently issued to us, and several cartridges that had misfired were found beside the dead; their lives may have depended upon those cartridges, so Major Routh, Ordnance Inspecting Officer, passed along the line.

IN EAST AFRICA

Dun, Smith, Allen and McQueen all down with fever. These of the officers, and the men in proportion. The climate is taking its toll.

On May 8th " D " Company had marched to hold Crater Hill, a strong position six miles east of Mzima, and on our Lines of Communication with Tsavo, a necessary step, for it was open for the enemy to occupy and " cut " our " lines," and it being a first-class defensive feature commanding the road, they would have required some ejecting from it.

Major Cashel at this time commanded the Mzima mobile column, and on May 13th became engaged with a force of Germans on the Mogiana River in " No Man's Land," and at the foot of Kilimanjaro. I cannot do better than write down, verbatim, the report rendered to me by Major Cashel on the action:—

To the O.C. Mzima Line, May 14th, 1915.

Sir,—I have the honour to report that I marched at 5.25 a.m. on May 12th, 1915, in accordance with instructions. I trekked in the direction of Kivokumi camp until 8 a.m., when I struck the spoor of two German scouts moving in that direction. I at once determined to move on to Maraba. I struck the Tsavo River at 9 a.m., and it took me an hour to get the donkeys and coolies across, the donkeys being the chief trouble. As I crossed below the junction of the Noturush and Tsavo Rivers I followed the former river up to Chitty's crossing and went over. The transport again took an hour to get across this small drift. I arrived at camp at Maraba at 5 p.m. and had some food cooked, trekked again at 8 p.m., and hid for the night in the bush. The donkeys took an hour to saddle and load, and gave considerable trouble on line of march by banging their boxes loudly against each other, and blocking the route. Distance covered, about 15 miles. Next morning I gave the men plenty of time to breakfast and get water, and trekked at 8 a.m., arriving at the Mogiana River by 12.20 p.m.; found no water in the river. Covered about 10 miles. Trekked to Tsavo River, and arrived about 1.45 p.m. just below old Kivokuki camp. I was here informed by the Transport Officer that he could not get his donkeys across the river, to where there was a good position. As the donkeys had had no water for some time, I determined to water, and let the men have food, and move across the river later, higher up.

I did not know I was near the crossing at the time, and was informed it was three miles further up. I noticed coming across the country that on the left bank of the Mogiana there is a road parallel to it, and about a quarter of a mile from it. The road is new but well beaten down. I saw another road between the Mogiana and Tsavo junction. This road is used daily by numbers of persons, and is beaten into a fine dust.

Enemy attacked my centre about 3.20 p.m. They then assailed the right, moved to the centre again, and then attacked the left. Some of them then crossed the river, but were easily beaten off by Capt. Coope. The enemy fired altogether about $2\frac{1}{4}$ hours, using his Maxims freely. When his left attack developed, the 2nd Rhodesian Regiment Maxims under Lieut. Tribe came into action, and took the heart out of the attack. The enemy moved off up the river as soon as his attack failed.

As I understood there was another body of Germans up the Rhombo River, I did not pursue, but proceeded to get my donkeys and transport across the river. The donkeys then took a still longer period to load up, and I had to start in the dark, which was an advantage in a way. Just after starting I was told that five men in all were missing. Had I been informed of this while I was in possession of the ground, I could easily have searched it while daylight lasted, but it would have been an impossible task in thick bush in the dark.

I did not feel justified in staying on the ground till the morning of May 14th and putting the column in danger of a heavy attack. I finally got the column off into the bush and started for Mzima. After about two hours going, I found the column had lost connection; this occurred through a man getting fast in a thorn, and instead of the next man going on, all waited and soon lost touch in the dense dark bush. I waited over an hour and heard the donkeys banging into one another and into the trees on my right flank about 300 yards off.

I sent twice over to the rear half of the column to come into touch, but could not get it done, and I finally went on. I trekked until 2 a.m., when I found it impossible to make any further way. My part of the column was three times charged by rhinoceros during the night, and various people were damaged slightly. One K.A.R. man was knocked senseless by being struck with a comrade's rifle. This morning I trekked at 5.20 a.m., and arrived in camp at 9 a.m. The rest of the column arrived safely about 10 a.m. I was seriously hampered in my movement by my transport, and had I been attacked heavily I should probably have lost it.

The chief cause of the trouble was the donkeys; they take too long to load; they bray occasionally; they make a noise going through the veldt, and they have great difficulty crossing a river except at a given point. They are most unsuitable for this veldt. It has been stated that they do not run away, but as the natives that control them do, and thereby let the donkeys calmly graze towards the enemy, this cannot be called an advantage. Capt. Woodward, Lieuts. Stokes and Frelinghaus and Capt. Ellis did excellent work, and I have already brought to your notice Capt. Coope and Lieut. Tribe, who were both of great assistance.

The following is a list of killed, wounded and missing :

2nd Rhodesia Regt., Killed,   735 Pte. J. Chaves.
                     ,,   728 Pte. E. Macrae.
                Wounded, 769 Sergt. Robertson.
130th Baluchis,   Wounded, 1326 Sepoy Saildallak.
                           ,,   1898 ,,   Dal Ruled.
Transport Dept., Missing, Cpl. R. Robertson.
                         ,,   Cpl. J. Campbell.
Intelligence Dept., Missing, Mr. A. Wadeson.
Ammunition expended : Maxim 2,000 rounds.
                        Per rifle, 60 rounds.

I have the honour to be, Sir,
Your obedient servant,

R. CASHEL, *Major*.
Commanding Mobile Column.

Mzima, May 14, 1915.

I have quoted word for word the above report, as it throws a light on the situation, represents symbolically many minor actions of a similar nature where patrol met patrol and fought indecisive actions.

It shows how donkey transport was used, because it was thought to be "fly-proof"—which it was not—and was found worse than useless.

It denotes the active defence of the Germans in assuming the offensive, for it was fought a mile from their camp; revealed months later. It indicates the difficulties of the line of march in dense thorn bush, in which the smallest incident may spell loss of cohesion and touch. Finally, it tells of a well-fought little action, in which the casualties would have been heavy had the enemy fired along the ground line instead of into the tree-tops; tells how Tribe, that matchless machine-gun officer—product of the B.S.A.P.—reserved the fire of his guns until the German Askari, answering the bugle-sound to charge, presented a target *en enfilade*, and how the assault withered and wilted under his directed fire. There is little room for criticism of the "affair of patrols." Major Cashel's patrol was surprised, but surprise in that bush was almost impossible to guard against. He might have stayed an hour and cleared up the ground after defeating the enemy's attack, and have turned an indecisive fight into a distinct success, but it must be remembered that he was unsupported; some 12 miles from Mzima; was probably within a mile of a strong enemy post, and in the presence of an enemy in touch with strong supports. It tells the tale of many small conflicts of like nature in "No Man's Land" in East Africa.

Yet it does not delineate lurid incidents that throw a ghastly glamour over this phase of the campaign in East Africa; perhaps they should not be spoken of because they are unspeakable, nor written of because unwriteable; but they must be referred to in order that the position may be understood, the ruthlessness of it appreciated. Such an incident will demonstrate the devilish brutality of the German troops in East Africa at this period. They wounded; then slew the wounded, the incapacitated, and the defenceless with bayonet and rifle butt. Having slain they stripped and mutilated, not merely by hacking and slashing, but with refined savagery, perpetrating such last offences and desecrations on the human body that normal mind could not conceive. The day following the affair on May 13th a party was sent to bury the dead by the Mogiana River. They interred the remnants of men, hacked, gashed and hideous. One who had worn long boots had had his legs disjointed and removed at the knees, but that atrocity paled beside the cruel indecencies wrought, and to which that burial party testified with horror in their eyes.

It is only fair and just to say here that as the campaign progressed these acts of barbarity became less in number, until from the middle of 1916 to the end of hostilities we faced a gallant and chivalrous enemy in the field, fighting with clean, ungloved hands.

" B " Company was still at Maktau, and on May 20th I received a letter from the Brigade-Major that the Regiment would be concentrated at Mzima, as it was considered the present storm centre; further, that Col. Vickers was being recalled to his regiment at Mombasa, and that I was to assume command of the Tsavo-Mzima line. The latter soon eventuated, but " B " Company still remained detached.

On May 20th Dunn took over " A " Company and Capt. Ogilvie resigned, Lieut. Smith being appointed Adjutant. On the 21st I took over the Tsavo-Mzima line, and the troop stationed thereon, namely, three Companies 2nd Rhodesia Regiment, four Companies 3rd Kashmir Rifles, two Companies 130th Baluchis, one Company 3rd K.A.R., two Companies 61st Pioneers, supply and transport service and a carrier corps.

The Mobile Column at Mzima is nominally 300 rifles and 2 Maxims, but it mustered 180 rifles only when turned out—the remainder were down with fever and dysentery.

Major Coope and Cashel were both very seedy, and I sent them peremptorily on three weeks leave; the men looked as thin as skeletons and worked to shadows. It was imperative for " C " Company to leave the stricken camp they had held so long ; on the day I took over, the Company was only 84 strong, and of these the M.O. returned 28 as sick and " No duty," and my diary says : " There is not a single officer without a cold, veldt sores, rheumatism, fever or dysentery." After a patrol I find I wrote the following in my diary that applies to this stage of the campaign : " This bush work is very trying for troops; rifles must be kept loaded, those of the flank and advance guards with safety-catches off. It is continual stopping and catching in thorns, listening to and for sounds ; momentarily expecting the crack of rifles at short ranges ; for hours hardly speaking in more than the lowest whisper ; the continual anxiety that some one may be losing touch ; all these combine to make this the most nervy and wearying class of fighting imaginable. No one who has not seen the bush of the Tsavo valley can understand it. Patterson in his book tried to describe it."

I found Cashel, Coope, Stokes, Frelinghaus, and " C " Company generally in such a low condition, so worn out with fever, dysentery and veldt sores that I packed them off for rest and change. They had done very well, and were relieved by " D " Company from Crater Hill, " A " Company relieving " D " at Crater.

Signal Hill was left alone, as being of no value to anyone. Our camp was removed from the Palm Grove swamp to the hill, a Union Jack was hoisted to show our enemy where we stood. Patrols were ordered to be of not less than one hundred strong, or not more than three. The one hundred with machine guns could hold their own with enemy patrols; the three, composed of one European and two native Askari, could go and creep anywhere, gathering and sending information. The hæmophrodite party of ten or twelve men wandering about aimlessly, or marching to a fixed point in " No Man's Land," was given up. They had cost too much in " regrettable incidents."

While three companies of the Regiment had been busy round Mzima, " B " Company at Maktau, under Capt. Coker, had not been idle. On May 20th they had been engaged in a small patrol encounter, and on June 5th in a more serious one towards the M'Buyimi ridge as part of the Maktau Mobile Column, in which Pte. Vernon was mortally, and Pte. Whitehead and Bruce severely, wounded. Here, L.-Corpl. Griffiths (later Lieut. Griffiths) held up the enemy until Lieut. Thomas with a small party supported him, and drove back a superior enemy force. Many little scraps came their way, and in all they did well, and the name of the Rhodesia Regiment along the Maktau-Voi line was in the safe keeping of " B " Company.

On the night of June 11th, telephone communications between Mzima and Crater camp were cut in three places, and contact mines of gun-cotton and dynamite were laid on the road—our carrier corps passed over them at daylight, but faulty laying and bad workmanship averted a disaster. On the 14th the Mzima Mobile Column returned from reconnaissance, and among other information brought back Lieut. Schultz's pocket-book, found on the crest of Longa-Longa, being a hill about nine miles west of Mzima. In it was a typewritten order signed by Von Lettow, the " General-Major " of the German forces, telling him to cut our telephone lines " before the contemplated attack on Mzima laager at daybreak on 15th." It seemed a providential find, and I sent out the Mobile Column to bivouac half-way between Mzima and Crater (whither I had sent rations) in order that on the attack materialising, it could operate independently against the flanks and rear of the enemy, whilst I held the position with 316 rifles, 4 machine-guns, and 2 trench mortars.

The attack did not come off, much to everyone's disappointment. That it was intended, was proved shortly afterwards, when a patrol stumbled on to a newly-cut road through the bush, fit for guns and transport, leading from Rhombo direction to within 1½ miles of Mzima post. Perhaps the loss of a pocket-book by Lieut. Schultz diverted it.

The weekly state shows 3 officers and 108 rank and file of the 2nd Rhodesia Regiment in hospital, and many others are sick in camp.

CHAPTER V.

I HAVE omitted to mention that on May 28th Major Cashel, Capt. Coope, Capt. Stokes, and Lieut. Frelinghaus, with the thin gaunt remnant of " C " Company, marched out of Mzima for a well-earned change at Bura—or Wusi, as it is sometimes called—a mountain sanitorium near Voi. Already the Indian troops treated the Rhodesians as comrades, and turned out with a sort of improvised band to speed them on their way. " D " Company arrived from Crater Hill on the same day, under Major Gordon, with Blagrove and Mitchell as subalterns. " A " Company relieved them at Crater, in turn to be relieved themselves on June 13th by a company of K.A.R., when they (" A " Company) marched into Mzima under Capt. Hare in time for and anticipating joyfully the expected attack that did not eventuate.

On June 17th a small event in itself, but almost a regimental disaster, occurred. It is entered in my diary as follows :— " Surgeon-Capt. Ellis has at last gone down with fever ; he has stuck conscientiously to his work, has been out with the Mobile Column every time it has gone in strength, and has done his arduous duty splendidly. He is always cheery under every circumstance (except an early cold breakfast !), and in fact he is invaluable in camps, mess, and field ; he has seen every officer—except myself and Blagrove—go down with some ailment before his turn has come." However, he remained on duty.

On the 19th, Major Cashel and Capt. Dunn returned looking very fit, and the former took over the Mobile Column from Capt. Woodward (130th Baluchis).

On the 22nd I received a wire : " In view of operations elsewhere, attacks in this neighbourhood may be expected in next few days." Well, by this time we were ready for them.

The Intelligence staff was not very efficient ; the natives would not budge without a white man, so Corpl. Reckenzaun and Pte. Bayliff took up the work, and did invaluable scouting, gleaning much information.

Little of importance was taking place now, in the theatre of war under our ken, except that the strategic railway was nearing Maktau. For the rest, indecisive patrol encounters occurred frequently, and the enemy blew up a bit of railway line here or surprised a bridge guard there.

I find the following entry in my diary for June 26th: "A welcome mail from Rhodesia arrived yesterday evening. A lot of comforts came on Thursday; they are so welcomed by the Regiment, and it is most extraordinary that they always seem to be the things most required and most welcome. A great deal of common sense must be used in their selection. Rhodesia is looking after her soldiers very well."

On June 27th the enemy made a long-range demonstration against Maktau, an entrenched and fortified camp; they fired some 500 rounds into it, and stampeded the crowd watching the 27th Mountain Battery detrain, but in all only wounded one Askari of the K.A.R.

I received a wire on June 21st that No. 912 Pte. Blamey had died of malaria in Voi hospital, and later I had a letter from his Company Officer, of which the following is an extract:—
"Poor old Blamey (he was always 'old' Blamey) died on the 20th after a long illness. He came in sick from Mzima, and just sank into a state of lethargy. Blamey was one of the men in the ambuscade when Signaller Wells and others were killed. It was Blamey who called out "Run for the lava," and those who could follow his advice were those who were saved that day. By this shall we always remember Blamey, but although the poor chap kept his head under those desperate circumstances, he never recovered from the shock."

Of No. 489 Pte. Passmore, who died at Voi at two o'clock on the morning of July 1st, I find written in my diary: "He was a most valuable man and a good comrade." Enteric claimed him.

At this time a well-known man of the regiment, Pte. Hart (62 years) used to patrol with two native scouts to the head waters of the Mzima river, where it bubbled out of the lava into a beautiful, still, palm-shaded pool. On July 1st he shot a rhinoceros which he stated had been in the habit of charging him daily, " and he couldn't stick it any longer."

Then L.-Corpl. Thorpe got lost on patrol, and my diary says the following action was taken: " Sent out six Intelligence native scouts to search for, and follow spoor of L.-Corpl. Thorpe. Sent a patrol from Crater Hill to patrol country east of it; Capt. Dunn and 100 men to patrol in widely-extended order, up and down either bank of Mzima River; right and left section pickets to extend their patrols to a three-mile radius; a patrol of 2nd Rhodesia Regiment and 4th K.A.R. to patrol to Rhodesia Hill (in rear of our lines). All sentries at the fort and Crater to look out for a signal fire lit by a man lost in the bush and report at once. Let us hope he will be found, it is an awful country for a greenhorn or a schoolmaster to be bushed in, and Thorpe is both." He was found, and came into camp after twenty-eight hours absence.

About this time the military situation again changed somewhat; the strategic railway had reached Maktau—this obviously a factor in our favour, for it threatened the German centre, although not vitally, thanks to our ability to concentrate troops quicker than he could withdraw his from his flanks to encounter us. It was necessary, therefore, for him to weaken his flanks and strengthen his centre. Our Intelligence soon acquainted us with the presence of a strong camp at Ziwani swamp, 20 miles north-west of Maktau, and only patrols in the direction of the hitherto entrenched camps at Rhombo and Kivokuni facing Mzima. The railway to Maktau had helped to equalise matters: hitherto the Germans had been able to feed their headquarters and centre at Moshi by rail, while we could not; now we could, and our own potential rapidity of closing on our centre was equal to theirs, and our extension to our flanks greater. We now held a tactical advantage, discounted only by the fact that our Lines of Communication were extremely vulnerable, possessing no alternatives; theirs being only lateral rail communication east with Tanga, and the alternative of falling back on the great central railway. We could possibly deal a blow at the body; they could strike at the heart.

Now followed an action that to the mere student and onlooker presents a problem difficult to unravel. The Mzima Mobile Column was ordered out to patrol actively towards Rhombo and Kivokuni on July 12th, 13th, and 14th, and it promptly set about doing so, although " A " and " D " Companies of the 2nd Rhodesia Regiment could parade only 75 men between them, 60 being sick in camp, including their C.O.'s, Capts. Gordon and Dunn. Big gun fire from the direction of Mbuyuni was heard on the 14th at Mzima from 9 a.m. to 9.20 a.m., and that evening I received a wire " No. 905 Pte. L. Martin killed, No. 718 L.-Corpl. Crook severely wounded; report follows."

The next entry in my diary for July 15th reads: " We learn that we attacked about 800 of the enemy at dawn at Mbuyuni yesterday. Enemy reinforced up to 2,000 by mid-day, our retirement ordered about 1.30 p.m. Our casualties 112, including 2 officers killed, 6 wounded. We are said to have punished the enemy heavily, and he did not pursue."

What necessitated this attack against a vastly superior force, superior in numbers and *morale*?—is the first question that springs to the mind of the uninitiated. To push the strategic railway 15 miles onward, lengthen our communication, dissipate our small force that was adequately protecting those lines? Surely these could not be quoted as reasons, and the only conclusion that the onlooker and student reaches is, that impatience and a desire " to do something " promoted an action that, had it been successful, would have meant little or nothing to us, whereas unsuccessful, it meant the strengthening of the already fine *morale* of the enemy.

There could be no military reason, tactical or strategical, for undertaking this hazardous attack on a known prepared position. Umbuyuni, the enemy position, was a low bush-crowned ridge 1,000 yards long, running roughly north and south, Maktau being 15 miles east of it; the eastern approach was across a dambo or vlei, 800 yards without cover other than baobab trees, which are not bullet-proof in spite of their being 12 to 18 feet in diameter. Our force consisted of about 900 rifles, 500 of which supported by two mountain guns were detailed to make a frontal attack over the open vlei, whilst 400 attacked the German left—two companies, " B " and " C," were merged in this. It is not clear why the frontal was the main attack, the enemy position was extended and narrow and difficult to organise in depth, in fact it was prepared for the very operation we conducted. Had the front held the Germans to their long line of " one-man " trenches, and a strong flank attack been developed, there would have been a chance of rolling them up. The frontal attack failed utterly, as might have been foreseen, and the flank attack was held up. The enemy was reinforced at mid-day and a retirement ordered at 1.30 p.m. The 29th and 30th Punjabis lost heavily in the abortive frontal attack. The Rhodesians lost No. 905 Pte. L. Martin (killed) and 718 Pte. F. D. Crook (severely wounded), both of " C " Company. The Germans displayed want of enterprise in not following up in pursuit of a signal victory thrust upon them. Resulting orders forthwith directed the two companies of the 2nd Rhodesia Regiment, (" A " and " D ") to the Voi-Maktau line, to be relieved at Mzima by the 2nd Kashmir Rifles.

The official *communiqué* published in the *Daily Leader* of B.E.A. on July 16th, 1915, commences : " On the morning of the 14th instant a column of all arms from Maktau under command of Brig.-Gen. Malleson proceeded to Mbuyuni, where it was known the enemy had placed a considerable force. The object of the move was to discover the enemy's strength and dispositions, as the activity of his patrols had recently prevented us from getting much information from this locality "; . . . and in bitter satire it concludes : " The success we attained is not out of proportion to the casualties inflicted upon us : total 35 killed, and about 120 wounded."

The above *communiqué* infers a " reconnaissance in force," and I think Napoleon spoke words to the effect that " a general who makes a reconnaissance in force usually gets what he deserves," and it was so in this instance.

On July 22nd Major Cashel with " A " and " D " Companies marched out of Mzima, destined for a health resort, Wusi, on the Voi-Maktau line, to enjoy a well-earned rest. I was ordered to remain behind to hand over Mzima post to Col. Hickson, K.A.R., and I retained Capt. Blagrove as my Staff-Officer. Seven poor fellows also remained, suffering from blackwater fever, the other sick having been sent on in batches beforehand. The officers and men of " A " and " D " were gaunt, yellow and emaciated, and many fell out of the ranks and had to be carried or sent to hospital on that short march to Tsavo, with a holiday in view in the hills of Wusi, which was reached on July 25th.

The next entry of interest that I find in my diary is : " On August 15th General Tighe, G.O.C., inspected Mzima line and post, and expressed his satisfaction, after which Lieut.-Col. Capell handed over command to Lieut.-Col. Hickson, commanding 4th K.A.R. On the 16th I left Mzima with Lieut. Blagrove (ex-B.S.A.P.), who has been acting Staff-Officer since July 9th, and excellently and efficiently he has done his work, more so even than the two officers of the Indian Army whom I had previously, and they were both good. I only mention this that general efficiency in all branches may be placed to the credit of the Regiment." We rejoined the Regiment at Bura, on the Voi-Maktau line, and glad we were to be " home " again.

The distribution of the Regiment on August 21st was "B " and " C " Companies at Maktau, " A " and " D " and headquarters at Bura. After dinner on the 20th the machine-gun officer of our comrades and friends the Loyal North Lancs Regiment, came over to the Officer's Mess. Both he and we had dined wisely and well, and a long bow was drawn probably by him, and Tribe of ours. At-long-last one or the other stated that his men could write their names on targets with a Maxim. This was beyond the limit, and I issued a challenge, eagerly accepted, for a competition between the two units in machine-gunnery ; the contest to embrace accuracy, rapidity and control of fire, number of hits on targets registered, tactical handling, and use of cover ; the whole to be adjudicated upon by officers of other and disinterested units. The match came off on the morning of August 21st, the 2nd Rhodesia Regiment beating the 2nd Batt. of the Loyal North Lancs on every point, and a pot of money changed hands, for the betting had been heavy amongst all ranks. I may say that we were filled with a justifiable pride at having beaten at their own game a crack regiment of the Imperial Army.

Orders had recently been issued for the 2nd Rhodesia Regiment to proceed to Kajiado. It was a welcome order, as for months the Regiment had not been together; yet in every action, in every pestilential locality, they had borne a share, if not more than a share. So, on August 22nd, 1915, " A " and " D " Companies left Bura at 1.30 p.m. " B " and " C " should have cleared Maktau at 11.30 a.m., but the enemy decreed otherwise, for within two miles of the post they blew up the engine intended for their train, which was being sent up from Voi.

In this connection I find in my diary the following entry.: " There was no engine in Maktau for us, and as one was steaming up from Voi, and had reached within two miles of Maktau, a tremendous explosion, visible from camp, occurred. Twenty-five mounted infantry were sent out (why not supported by 200 infantry I don't know) to endeavour to cut off the party that had blown up the line. It was known to be a considerable force, as bugles had been heard sounding. About four miles out the mounted infantry gained touch with the enemy, consisting of about 35 mounted Europeans and 70 Askari. The mounted infantry were too weak to do anything but fire a few shots and return to camp. Investigation proved the mine to have been well and truly laid, exploding under the front wheel of the engine, and throwing it with its tender and two trucks off the line. There was evidently leakage of intelligence from the camp to the German lines. The 2nd Rhodesia Regiment had struck tents and packed up over night, and in ordinary course would have been in the front train on the line in the morning; fortunately there was no engine in Maktau, and one had to be sent up from Voi, and it instead of us sustained the injury. The intention of the enemy evidently was to derail our train and decimate us as we scrambled out of the carriages, and then to disappear into the bush unharmed.

By August 25th the Regiment was concentrated at Kajiado, once more in general reserve. On the 27th we were required to find a post at the 56-mile peg on the line between Kajiado and Lake Magadi, and Lieut. Thomas left with 17 rank and file of " B " Company for the purpose. On the same date the officers of the 25th Royal Fusiliers dined with us, including that great Rhodesian and hunter, Capt. Selous, hale and hearty as a boy in his sixtieth (?) year.

We had brought eight horses up from Rhodesia, and had left them in Nairobi while we soldiered in the fly-struck pestilential country surrounding Mzima and Maktau; now we regained them and a few other old hairy remounts, and on off days the officers would get mounted and chase the game that abounded in the Kajiado area. A zebra, vildebeeste, eland, oryx, or some particular individual of a species would be marked down and singled out for a glorious run over veldt, through bush, by hill and dale. But death did not grimly accompany the sport: just a camera or two portrayed the scene and the panting quarry, and the hunt was ended and the animal free to rejoin his mates and tell them that all sport is not killing.

On such a pursuit the officers embarked on September 8th, a glorious morning for a ride. A troop of giraffe was found a mile from camp, and a grand old female singled out and separated from the herd. For mile after mile she loped along in ungainly gait, but covering the ground at a great pace; the country was broken—it was flat, it was hilly; dale, dell and plain alternating—but gallop one must for a near view of the splendid creature. Horse and man throbbed and panted, clothes were torn to shreds in particles of bush. " Will it never end ? " thought some; " May it last for ever ! " said others. No one with a spark of sportsman's instinct would have pressed a trigger on the magnificent animal that gave in at the end of a ten-mile point; and she seemed to know it, standing composed but anxious in our midst, as we photographed her splendid form, dappled brown and yellow. Perhaps her temper changed at some taunt thrown carelessly at her—some disparaging remark touching the length of her neck or the pose of her small head, for of a sudden she fixed an angry eye on Tribe, sitting his horse some ten or twelve yards distant. Tribe caught that glance and turned his steed, and at the same moment the spotted beauty strode swiftly forward, and with a lightning-like lift of a long fore-leg, landed a loud, resounding blow on a helmeted head. Tribe, executing a double parabola in mid-air, fell unconscious on the sward. The great cloven hoof descended on the rump of the staggering horse, the big giraffe strode from our midst, and I know our impulse was to give her a cheer. Tribe was picked up and carried to the shade of a bush, and as Prohibition had not been introduced into East Africa, was soon brought to consciousness. The terrified horse galloped ten miles to Kajiado, and died the following day.

And the rest—and the sport, and the play—was well earned by men who had stared anxiety fraught with danger in the face for months, never knowing from moment to moment, by night or by day, when the solitary crack of a mauser would herald an engagement. A march through the bush with column or patrol was nerve-racking work for officers, especially for the commander, for he could not see ahead ; scouts were of little use, and always through the long hours of march he was planning, planning—framing his dispositions in case of attack by, or contact with, an unseen enemy ; momentarily, as hill, donga, spruit or kopje was reached or passed, his scheme must alter, and at any second through the long day or dreary night that rifle report might stir him from his kaleidoscopic scheming, calling on him to put his latest and present thought into quick action. Nerves stretched to breaking-point caused many breakdowns, and doubtless induced disease and sickness, which ever kept us company.

CHAPTER VI.

RHODESIA was doing her best to keep her Regiment up to strength, 25 men arriving on August 13th; 93 on October 12th, and 200 on November 4th, this draft recruited principally in the Union of South Africa. All were of a good hard stamp, fit for service anywhere, with a fair sprinkling of experienced old soldiers amongst them; well selected and almost ready to take the field, for they had been in training under Capts. New and Blatherwick of the British South Africa Police, in Salisbury—officers to whom the Regiment owed much. Yet all drafts arriving were put through a course of musketry, and a three-weeks' course of drill before being "passed"; it was necessary that they should acquire the tone and the "quiffs" and tenor of the Regiment, that it might be an entity, combined in every movement, thinking almost one thought.

Except for hard and daily training, the Regiment settled down to enjoy what appeared to be a holiday—its sole charge the line of rail and posts culminating at the Magadi soda lake, that dazzling expanse of snow-white alkali. Incidentally it was being held in general reserve. Game, both great and small, furred and feathered, was plentiful; heavy bags were made, hair-raising encounters with *feræ naturæ* related over Nazareth's pewter pots.

On Saturday, September 11th, Capt. Coker and I visited Lieut. Thomas's camp at 56-mile post, near where a lion of evil tendencies, and a reputed man-eater, prowled. Several of the men joined in a hunt, and we beat up a dry river bed, in which the spoor of a mighty male lion was deeply imprinted in the sand. Ah! those thrilling moments of a lion hunt—equalled only on the blood spoor of a wounded buffalo—when the next second or two may call upon you to face a roaring, hurtling demon. Near the end of the beat we were making was a patch of thick bush and undergrowth; some hunters were beating down towards it, others waiting for the brute to break, when an ominous deep-throated growl sounded from the thicket; it gave pause to all, for the bush was tangled and dense. Yet Thomas on his pony trod on forbidden ground, and the great tawny bulk of a male maned lion made a rush towards him, but turned quickly and retired to his impenetrable lair. Lieut. Thomas, followed by low angry growls, emerged from that shady river bed into the blazing scorching sunlight, with an appearance of having seen the very Devil himself.

So a council was held, it being manifestly impossible to dislodge *felix leo* by ordinary means. Finally it was decided to get some Indian soldiers at a hard-by post to fire the grass from the lower end of the river bed, whilst riflemen took up likely positions. The grass and tousled undergrowth burned and crackled finely, and soon with a mighty roar the lion broke cover: rifles cracked and bullets spattered round his galloping form, but he held on, tail erect as a terrier-chased cat, and uttering a low rumbling growl. Luck and the lion came my way; previous experience had told me his genus will usually make for a rock-strewn hill if there is one in sight, and on such a one I took my post, with Thomas. The lion came bravely on as though he would crest the hill over the boulders a hundred yards on my left, so I ran as hard as the nature of the ground would permit to shorten the distance. As I got to within forty yards of the spot I reckoned he should appear, out he burst, trotting with long slow paces. My ·375 bullet struck him fair and square, but beyond uttering a nasty grunt he seemingly took no notice. So the hunt foregathered and took up the spoor, advancing cautiously in expectation of a savage charge; but our splendid quarry lay dead fifty yards from where he got the bullet, shot from shoulder to shoulder.

All that mars the memories of that day is the thought that more than one of those fellows, full of health, strength and the love of sport and war, have "gone West," while others are dangling shattered and broken limbs, maimed beyond repair.

But at this time, although game was teeming in the country, men who rested after hard fighting, and strenuous work for the Empire, and particularly for British East Africa, were forbidden even to ride game down, not for killing, but for photography—had to obtain permission to shoot a lion, which was granted if it was savage, or molested cattle, and were grudgingly allowed to kill a buck on special permit signed and dated by a Staff-Officer.

On Thursday, September 16th, information was received confidentially that an attack was to be made on Longido by troops under Col. Jolly. "A" and "D" Companies were ordered to Bissel to act as reserve, and left under command of Capt. Dunn, together with two machine-guns under Sergt. Blair.

Only one officer—Capt. McQueen—of the 2nd Rhodesia Regiment took part in the raid on Longido just referred to—he earned there a Military Cross. It would appear that from 200 to 300 mounted men and some King's African Rifles attacked for some reason or other the strong and entrenched position—only we who had occupied it knew *how* well-entrenched, *how* strong—of Longido, garrisoned by some 400 of the enemy. The result was veiled in mystery, and as little as possible talked about : we only heard through unofficial sources that 6 of the gallant East African Mounted Rifles were killed, 31 equally brave Askari wounded. Later that our wounded totalled 62, enemy's loss slight ; 17th Cavalry (Indian) not engaged. Lieut. Col. Jolly's District Command Orders on the engagement did not come to our notice, if any were published.

We heard nothing of the affair officially, but a sentence in my diary reflects the thoughts of the troops, just the ordinary fighting-men at the time ; it reads : " Surely someone will be Stellenbosched."

Capt. Dunn with " A " and " D " Companies return to Kajiado on September 27th. In spite of the rest and sunny climate and high altitude, the sick report of October 9th shows 2 officers and 110 rank and file in hospital, and 29 attending sick parades.

6.30 p.m., Friday, October 15th : Regiment ordered to coast ; rolling stock arriving 1.30 a.m., immediate entrainment.

8.30 p.m., altered to Voi.

9.30 p.m., " As you were." All tents had been struck and the Regiment packed ready to leave ; presumably false alarm.

Cricket and football took place regardless of season. On October 17th the Officers 2nd Rhodesia Regiment played the Sergeants of the Regiment. Win for Officers : scores 176-135, a very good match. Blagrove and Hare, Sergts. Cookson and Cranswick did good batting. Frielinghaus bowled very well.

On the same date the Regiment played the remainder of the Garrison at Soccer, winning by 3 goals to nil.

Sunday October 24th, Officers and N.C.O.'s of Regiment play Privates at cricket and win by 20 runs.

Here we met the 3rd Kashmir Rifles under Capt. Money. They are mostly Gurkhas—cheery, irresponsible little fellows. The Commanding Officer and his native officers are soon counted as staunch friends, and remain so to the end, sharing many hardships, and standing side by side on several shot-swept fields, from Kajiado to Rufigi.

My diary of October 30th says : " On Monday we send a team to Nairobi to play united British East Africa and Uganda on the Monday, and combined Nairobi and Mombasa on Tuesday ; if we win it may well be conceded that Rhodesia has beaten the two Protectorates." And November 3rd says : " Rugby team returned from Nairobi ; they won Monday's game by 25 points to 3, and Tuesday's by 17 points to nil ; our team played splendidly, but was never really extended."

Yes ! Rhodesia has writ her name large in East Africa ; and there stands a ragged bush-clad hill two miles east of Mzima, charted on the maps of the country, to be known and written of, perhaps, for ages as " Rhodesia Kop " ; and within her shadow Rhodesians will for ever lie buried where they fell in glorious but unequal combat.

Marching Orders ! and the Regiment entrained on November 10th for Maktau ; arrived there on the 11th, relieving the 25th Royal Fusiliers, and were cordially met and entertained by the 130th K.G.O. Baluchis and 4th King's African Rifles, old and well-tried friends.

At Maktau we find an army in the making, being slowly fashioned into a concrete form ; aeroplanes, armoured cars, and 4-inch Naval guns from the ill-starred *Pegassus*—all lend a hopeful and cheery aspect to the situation.

My diary for November 15th says : " Camp inspection to-day ; only complaints received, against fleas ; they certainly swarm, but must be considered as ordinary adjuncts to active service conditions. Lieut. McCarthy parades his fleas for inspection to-morrow, he being a complainant ! ! ! "

Wednesday, November 17th, Officers and N.C.O's practise bomb-throwing : Col.-Sergt. Harris, overwhelmed by curiosity and anxiety to witness the result of his projectile, bobbed up over the cover from behind which we threw, and received a slug in the shoulder ; fun, laughter and chaff were his only solace for a fairly severe wound, and serve him right.

On the night of November 18th-19th, it became " B " Company's turn to find a fore laying party, to surprise enemy parties molesting our line of rail near Maktau. About midnight a party of about 50 put in an appearance, and a little fire fight by night ensued, the armoured train steaming up and taking part ; the enemy cleared out, and morning revealed one dead German Askari, with a bag full of fuzes and explosives.

Sunday, 28th : 2nd Rhodesia Regiment played the garrison at Rugby and won by 16 points to 3 ; it was a very rough game, but when made necessary, we can play that too."

On Sunday, December 5th, a patrol returned from the

direction of Mbuyuni reporting that position unoccupied, and on the 6th, railway construction to the west recommenced.

Then, on December 7th, 200 2nd Rhodesia Regiment were ordered to Maungu by rail to operate from there, together with 500 of the 130th Baluchis, against Kasigau—a position within thirty miles of the rail, lately captured by the enemy. They went, but do not seem to have effected anything in particular, beyond enduring a very hard time, with a shortage of water and the necessaries of life, and returned to Maktau on December 12th.

The necessity for the movement of troops above referred to seems rather obscured, and the available information to the uninitiated may be summed up in the entry in my diary: " Little is clear except that about 40 K.A.R. fought about 1,000 Germans, with 3 quick-firing guns and several Maxims, for many hours : then broke up and retired on Maungu : they evidently made a very gallant stand, Lieut. Kenyon Slaney commanding. A force of about 1,000 rifles was then collected under Lieut.-Col. Graham, of 3rd K.A. Rifles, but ultimately it was not considered strong enough to attack Kasigau with ; our contingent of 200 Rhodesians under Major Cashel formed part of this Force. The project was abandoned. The railway and communications are now being strongly held, and I presume the Germans are being left in possession of Kassigau : and why not ? We can pass Union reinforcements round it to Maktau, and then when we are strong enough Kasigau will be cut off, unless the enemy vacate it."

About this time, ten native scouts are sent up from Rhodesia, and are placed under Corpl. Guiney, a fearless scout himself ; they remained, less two killed in action, until the last, doing invaluable work for the Regiment.

The Air Service, as at December 18th, 1915, in East Africa was not in our eyes highly efficient, as the following entry denotes : " Another aeroplane fallen and come to grief, pilot uninjured ; this leaves us five out of the eight we started with, it would appear they are most unreliable"

Followed the Regiment's first Christmas away from home, far from sunny Rhodesia. But on Christmas morn arrived Rhodesia's presents—thirty-eight packing cases stuffed with good things : and as I had been able to get some beer up from Voi, and because Rhodesians fought well and successfully in the boxing contests held on Christmas night, the day was enjoyed by all. Appended are extracts from Special Orders of the day.

2ND RHODESIA REGIMENT.

ORDERS DATED December 24th, 1915 :—

No. 78. SEASON'S GREETINGS.—The following wire has been received from the Commandant-General, Rhodesia, reading— " Compliments of the season to you all. My warmest congratulations to the Regiment on having gained the fine reputation it has and my best wishes to you all for success in the coming year."

The following wire was sent to the Administrator, Salisbury, from 2nd Rhodesians, reading :—" Members of the 2nd Rhodesia Regiment send greeting to your Honour and the people of Rhodesia." This latter wire was sent previous to the receipt of the former.

After Order by Lieut.-Colonel A. Essex Capell, D.S.O., dated December 24th, 1915.

No. 79. SEASON'S GREETINGS.—The following wire has been received from the Administrator, Salisbury, Rhodesia, reading as follows : " To O.C. Rhodesian Regiment, Maktau. Cordially reciprocate your kindly greetings and wish you and all the Regiment a Merry Christmas. I congratulate you most heartily on the excellent reputation the Regiment has earned."

The above wire was dated at Salisbury, December 24th, 1915.

The following is an extract taken from 2nd Rhodesia Regiment Orders dated December 27th, 1915 :—

No. 80. SEASON'S GREETINGS.—The following wire was received from Salisbury on December 24th, 1915, from the President and Directors, B.S.A.Co. " O.C. Rhodesians, Maktau. Best wishes for Christmas and New Year and congratulations on good work done."

The following reply was sent : " Hearty reciprocations, so much to do, so little done."—2nd Rhodesians.

The following wires were received and replied to on December 25th, 1915 :

" Greetings and best of luck."—E.A.M.R.

" O.C. Rhodesians, Maktau. Hearty Christmas to you all.—Rev. Soutter."

No. 81. K.A.R. CHRISTMAS FUND.—The following letter has been received from Mrs. H. Graham, dated December 23rd, 1915 :—

" Dear Colonel Capell,—Will you thank all of those in the 2nd Rhodesia Regiment for their very generous contribution to the K.A.R. Christmas Fund ? It is simply splendid of them to have even thought of subscribing. Our men will be so pleased when they are told of the compliment paid them by your Regiment."

A cheque for Rs. 505·50 cents was handed to the Hon. Sec. by the Paymaster on December 23rd, 1915, this being the amount subscribed by the Regiment.

The following is a letter received from Lieut.-Colonel B. R. Graham : " My dear Capell,—Very many thanks for your kind letter and a copy of the Order which go to my wife to-day. I had not written myself as the Christmas Fund idea emanated with my wife and she has been running it on her own. Hope she won't turn Suffragette later ! May I take the opportunity of adding to her thanks the very sincere gratitude of all ranks of the 1st, 3rd and 4th King's African Rifles, not only for the very generous gift, but also for the kindly thought which prompted it. May I say I think it is one of the most charming compliments I have ever known paid by British troops to their coloured brethren. May 1916 be a fizzis for you all."

No, really, the Aboriginal Protection Society need not perturb itself; the actions and feelings of the Regiment were only symbolical of Rhodesia's attitude towards natives, inculcated under a Chartered Company's rule.

On the afternoon of December 27th, a helio was observed twinkling from the bush, and it flashed the news that a force of the 25th Royal Fusiliers from Bura were stranded in the bush without food or the possibility of getting to any. Lieut. Frielinghaus with twenty-five 2nd Rhodesia Regiment left with porters carrying rations and marched on a compass bearing through dense bush—a march more difficult to effect in such surroundings by day than one by night of similar distance in a fairly open country. He did a fine march, and found the famished Fusiliers about daylight on the 28th. Fortunately they had water, as they had chanced upon a German supply depot, with water-drums and calabashes, and a deserted camp; this had evidently served as an intermediate base for the raiding parties that frequently to our confusion and surprise crossed the waterless tract to interfere with our railways, bomb our locomotives, and place explosives on our lines. The water must have been conveyed by carriers some twenty miles.

An aeroplane went up on December 30th with the intention of bombing Mbuyuni and Serengetti camps; it attained a great height, then "crashed," landing in the bush and smashing itself up; fortunately the pilot was unhurt. The planes seemed quite useless, unreliable, and disappointing, as much faith had been placed in their 100-lb. bombs, charged with 70-lb. T.N.T.

On January 12th Belfields' Scouts, accompanied by Corpls. Guiney, Ledingham, Clack, and Pte. Bayliffe, reconnoitred Serengetti Camp and found it held in strength.

Our railway was being pushed slowly but surely onwards towards the enemy, the covering troops to the working parties having almost daily skirmishes with the enemy; on January 18th, Campi-ya-Bibi, six miles west of Maktau, was occupied and established as rail-head, and an entrenched camp made.

Water from a reservoir constructed in the Bura Hills some 30 miles away was brought by a pipe-line, and all ranks were put on a ration of two gallons per diem as from January 20th, to be reduced to one gallon per man for all purposes on January 21st. Think of it, reader !—you use more daily before you sit down to your breakfast, you pour that amount into your washbasin to rinse your hands in!

By the evening of January 21st, 1916, the Brigade had mobilized at Campi-ya-Bibi preparatory to an attack on Mbuyuni on the morrow, and the 5th S.A. Infantry marched into camp, the first Union troops to arrive.

The operation against Umbuyuni was commenced by the advance guard starting at 4.30 a.m. on January 22nd. It was composed of one battalion 2nd Rhodesia Regiment, 130th Baluchis, 28th Mountain Battery, No. 1 Light Battery, one company Belfields' Scouts, and one company Mounted Infantry under my command. A frontal attack would appear to have been decided upon, but having no inside information I am uncertain if this was so, for the Umbuyuni ridge was held lightly by the enemy—4 whites and about 50 Askari—who were easily pushed out of it, leaving 1 officer and 5 Askari killed. The advance guard passed on over the Mbuyuni ridge and took up position 1½ miles in advance, whilst the main body consolidated the position. The enemy attacking the advance guard pluckily, but lightly, in flank caused some confusion, during which the Baluchis with a cheer, charged " F " Company 2nd Rhodesia Regiment under Blagrove, who danced round blowing his whistle, trying to make them understand they were " off-side." The attack dwindled, and only one man of " F " Company was hit.

The next day the potentiality of armoured cars acting in open grass country was put to the test. They (two)—with the Mounted Infantry (one company) and the Light Battery, with the 130th Baluchis—acted as a protective force west of camp. Encountering a body of about 40 enemy infantry, the Mounted Infantry, under Capt. Atkinson, of the Loyal North Lancs, gave chase and " turned them." The armoured cars then went slap into them, and nearly all were killed, wounded or taken prisoners. My impression of the moment is outlined in my diary thus : " Those armoured cars are irresistible, huge Rolls-Royce machines, heavily armoured, four tons of silent-night and noiseless engines, bounding over the veldt, over bush and stump, through brushwood and grass, into the midst of a body of infantry, where they begin to spit fire and bark bullets, themselves invulnerable—as a khaki-clad Juggernaut they ride over those that resist, shoot down those that run. There is no reason why two such cars in open country should not entirely destroy a whole battalion, provided their ammunition lasted out. We are very glad the Germans have none ; a car with a pom-pom or light Hotchkiss would seem to be their antidote and bugbear."

In miniature it is very near to the story of the tank that came into being at a later date.

I will further quote the entries in my diary for a few days.

Monday, January 24th, 1916: "Whole Brigade, less 130th Baluchis and 61st Pioneers, marched out against Serengetti, which was reported as occupied. The 2nd Rhodesia Regiment again formed the advance guard. Serengetti was bombarded with ranging fire only, when the Rhodesians, Belfields' Scouts, and two armoured cars were thrown forward on to the position to draw fire. The approach was over a treeless, open, sloping glacis, but no fire spat from the perfectly-concealed trenches, and we eventually discovered the position had been evacuated the day before; the body of Germans we cut up yesterday evidently having been protective troops covering the withdrawal. The enemy camp comprised miles of beautifully constructed trenches, enclosing a couple of square miles, and easily accommodating 5,000 men; communication trenches made a network throughout the whole, by which troops could be moved unseen to any threatened portion of the perimeters. The 130th Baluchis were sent to occupy the position in the evening. Water has to be conveyed there by motor trolley from our pipe here."

January 25th: "The first train steamed into camp (Mbuyuni) this afternoon. Still on one gallon of water per diem, and clean baths are only dreamt-of luxuries; officers give half a gallon each per diem to Mess for cooking, tea, coffee, washing-up, etc., and keep half gallon for washing and cold drinks. One has to adopt a certain routine and get a storage vessel of some kind, so that hand and face washing water if conserved for two days will on the third provide a small but dirty bath, which in turn becomes clothes washing water. But no one minds, for we are getting on with it."

On the 27th two of our aeroplanes passed over from Maktau to bomb Taveta. One effected its object, the other fell about a mile west of Serengetti, which we are now holding, occupying the well-planned German camp. As it planed down the enemy shot at it heavily, but failed to hit the pilot; when it settled they took cover, evidently apprehensive of the powers of the great bird on the ground—the German Askari has named the aeroplane "the bird that lays the iron egg." A double company of 130th Baluchis went out and burnt the remains of it. A rather good riddance of an unreliable machine, which has nearly broken down on previous occasions.

The South African Regiments, 5th and 6th S.A.I., had very fair bands with them—drum, bugle and bagpipe—and played every evening, the 5th giving a concert on February 2nd. It is a moot point whether bands are justifiable on active service; personally, I am of opinion that they are, provided they can be financed, do not minimise the numbers of fighting troops, have been trained in musketry, and are available for defensive purposes. If they serve to keep troops in good heart and spirit they are invaluable on a hard and dreary campaign, and should be maintained until the moment of marching into action.

The South African regiments seemed to our little Rhodesian unit as those fostered and cherished—with transport unlimited, where ours was curtailed to barest necessities; tents in plenty, where we had no shelter; a band, where we had no bugle; comforts, where we had bare existence. There was only one essential or non-essential in which they did not surpass the Rhodesians: namely, " heart "—or, as General Buller dubbed it, " guts."

CHAPTER VII.

FOLLOWING on the little events recorded in the last chapter, came preparations for an operation seemingly on a larger scale. Salaita, the German advanced post, stood on the road between us and the strong position of Taveta and headquarters at Moshi. Patrols were despatched to feint in this direction and that, and bloody little encounters ensued.

The 5th S.A.I. on February 7th march by night to round up the enemy post at Luchoro, 15 miles south-west of Serengetti, lose their direction in the bush and darkness, and return to camp at daybreak.

The 2nd Rhodesia Regiment, supported by the 130th Baluchis, is ordered to demonstrate towards Salaita on the same date.

Just east of the Ngoro spruit drift, four miles west of Serengetti, I posted the 130th Baluchis and the 28th Mountain Battery to act as a support, or as a reinforcement if circumstances necessitated. I procured as guide an officer of the 130th Baluchis, who had at one time during a former operation caught a glimpse of Salaita, and owned to a hazy idea of its whereabouts. Considerable sniping from the trees fringing the Nogto spruit took place, but as we crossed some four miles north of the drift, it was overcome by searching fire, and we marched on through thick but not dense bush. Of a sudden we burst from the forest into fairly open country, and to the astonishment of our guide and ourselves, Salaita Hill, strong and forbidding, rose before us 1,500 yards distant. Two flags, the German Eagle and the Mahommedan Crescent on its green ground, floated bravely from the fortress on its crest. Porters were observed carrying ammunition down the steep slopes to the trenches sited below, probably in the narrow fringes of scrub, bush and rocks that nearly encircled the position, rendering splendid cover from view, and opportunity for fashioning concealed obstacles against attack. General activity could be observed in the stronghold, but not a shot was fired from it.

To attack the position with the 350 rifles at my immediate command would have been futile, and not within the scope of my instructions. We had placed ourselves in a somewhat

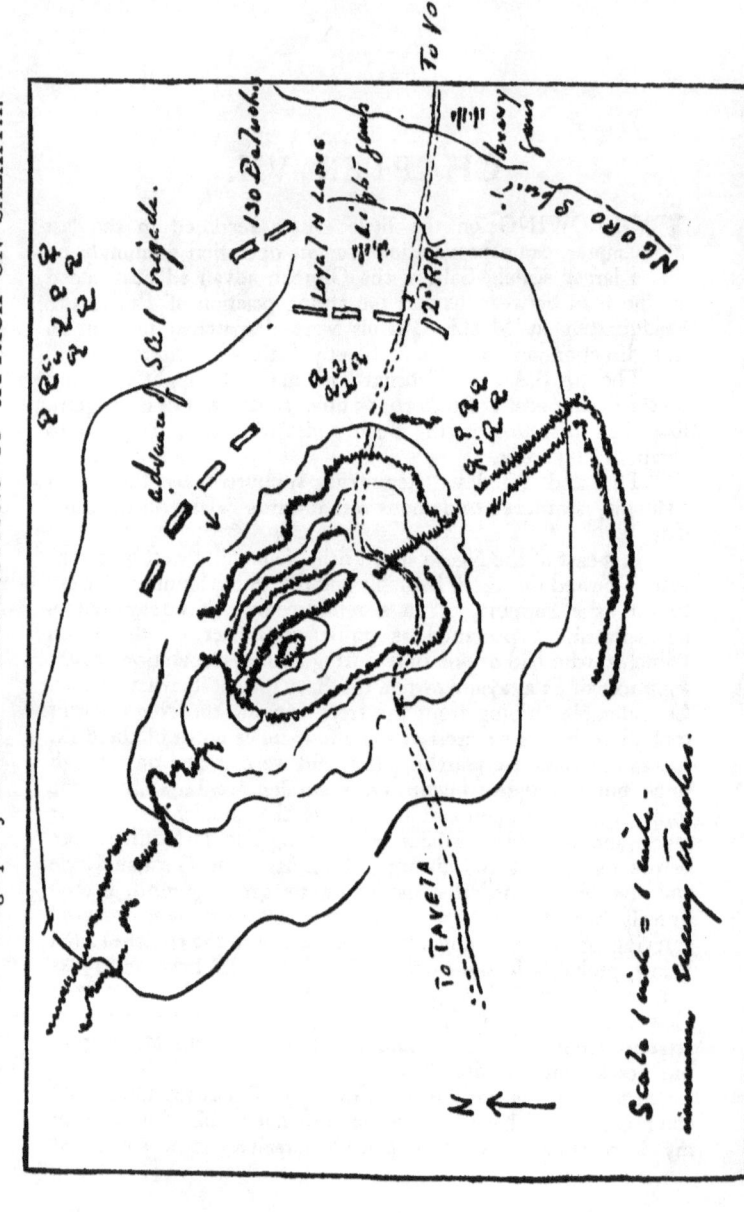

DISPOSITIONS OF ATTACK ON SALAITA.
12 February, 1916.
From Aerial Photograph of Salaita.

precarious position, for should the enemy be holding the ridge west of the Ngoro, and be also in strength at Salaita, we were in danger of being sandwiched between the two forces.

So I moved the Regiment to a little south of the Serengetti-Salaita road, and commenced to withdraw from a rather uncomfortable position. We had not gone far when firing opened on us from the ridge west of Ngoro, at about 900 yards range. Our machine-guns came into action at once, and the ridge was seen to be only lightly held by some 30 of the enemy, who were soon on the run in a southerly direction. As they crossed an open patch they fell down like ninepins, and I personally saw several very plucky actions, the wounded being carried away by comrades under an intense fire. Meanwhile an attack was developing in our rear, and Salaita being only 2,000 yards away, a heavy one was anticipated. Such was not the case, only about 50 Askari were observed, and the volume of fire denoted about this number. Capt. Jesser-Coope, in command of the rearguard, was able to cope with them without asking for reinforcements; their fire was silenced, they were driven off, and the march continued.

The enemy shooting had been wild, and our only casualty was Lieut. Dennis, of the Intelligence Department, who had accompanied the reconnaissance, which had at least served one purpose, namely, to show that the enemy's trenches were sited at the base of Salaita Hill, probably in the fringe of bush surrounding it. Not until Friday, February 11th, were orders for the attack on Salaita issued, and the 1st E.A. Brigade and 2nd S.A. Brigade moved to Serengetti. The orders were briefly that the 2nd S.A. Brigade should initiate the attack from the north, the Artillery and E.A. Brigade to develop the attack later from the east.

At daybreak on the 12th, the 2nd Rhodesia Regiment moved off on the right of the column, until Ngoro spruit was crossed, when the S.A. Brigade detached to open the attack. A mile west of this point our artillery came into action; it consisted of two 4-inch Naval guns (H.M.S. *Peggy*), 5-inch howitzers, Calcutta Battery, and Logan's Light Battery, and fired at a range of about 3,000 yards.

The German flag and the Mahomedan Crescent still floated over the citadel. The fire was for the most part directed to the crest of the hill, and possibly throughout the bombardment the enemy did not suffer a casualty. The Germans replied with some light but high-velocity long-range guns—probably the second armament of the *Köningsberg*—and made excellent practice on the fine target we presented. A heavy fire could be heard from north of Salaita, denoting the South Africans' attack, German machine-gun and pom-pom fire predominating. The Loyal North Lancs and the 2nd Rhodesia Regiment were then thrown forward to attack from the east as arranged; a heavy shell-fire met them, and they lay on the ground for more than an hour with a blazing sun streaming down on their backs, waiting for the flank attack to develop, subjected to heavy shell and searching rifle fire. The Brigade-Major came anon and ordered the regiment to advance 500 yards. I demurred, and asked for orders in writing, for we held a fair position with a fine field of fire, whereas if we went forward 500 yards we should be in a vlei swept by commanding Salaita. At the same time I sensed the tide of battle by the sound of the firing moving round to our right rear; it was plain that the flank attack had failed, that they were retiring, and the further we moved forward the more our flank would be uncovered and the more we should be enveloped in the then inevitable retirement. A few minutes later the Brigade-Major (Mainprice) came to me and said: "You were quite right, for the flank attack has left you somewhat in the lurch; they are beaten back, and retiring to your right rear." So we sent back 100 men as gun escort; the Loyal North Lancs were withdrawn, and we were left in the air, as a very much detached rear-guard. In short, disaster stalked abroad, but the ground must be held till all others were clear, till all others were re-organized behind us. Men of two broken regiments streamed through our ranks, running to the rear, getting to safety, and yet Rhodesians lay there quietly shooting when targets offered, quietly enduring a shell-fire that our guns had failed to silence, and then failed to reply to. For a few anguish-stricken minutes I lost touch with my men—almost doubted, and wondered if they would stay staunch in the presence of such frailty. A panic-stricken man passed by, wild-eyed, stripped of equipment, a phantom of terror; he passed close to a private of the Rhodesians, who looked up from his smoking rifle to the other's affrighted face, and cheerily shouted: "Hi, where are you going, mate?" In that instant, and once and for all, I caught and held the spirit of the gallant Rhodesian Regiment, never to be doubted again, always to be relied on in the bitterest extremities. Yes! as an army retired beaten, it only asked: "Where are you going, mate?"—and held on.

When the army was re-organized and guns were marshalled safely in rear, the Rhodesians rose from the stricken field, and turned reluctant backs upon an enemy; and at the Ngoro spruit passed through the gallant Baluchis who were there to assume the duties of rear-guard. Almost at that moment the right flank of that splendid native regiment was heavily attacked, they seem hard pressed; we offered assistance to our old comrades of many scraps—to the Indian soldiers we respected and almost loved—but their gallant commander, Major Dyke, preferred to fight his fight unaided; won through, and that same night found time to write: " My dear Colonel, I should like to thank you all for the very kind expressions of good-will that were made about us by a number of your officers. Both our officers and men have the greatest affection for the Rhodesians, and we wish for no better fellows on our side, whether in victory or reverse." This ready appreciation of our friendship was followed on the morrow by a parade of the Indian officers of the regiment presenting me with an almost historic document, that read: " To the Officers, rank and file of the 2nd Rhodesia Regiment (through the O.C., 2nd Rhodesia Regiment). Respected Sir,—We, the Indian Officers and rank and file of the 130th Baluchis, having come to know this morning when fall in for parade, from our Officer Commanding, that all the Officers, rank and files of your Regiment requested heartily to the G.O.C. for our help when yesterday we were surrounded by the enemies: Pay our best and hearty thanks for your this sympathetic kindness and militarism, we hope for the future that we all will side by side to each other. We pray to our Heavenly Father for the victory of our Government. May God it be soon. We are, your best sympathetic, I. O., R. and F. of 130th Bal."

Oh, East is East, and West is West, and never the twain shall meet,
Till earth and sky stand presently at God's great Judgment-seat;
But there is neither East nor West, Border, nor Breed, nor Birth,
When two strong men stand face to face, tho' they come from the ends
   of the earth.—*Kipling*.

And thus a blood brotherhood, tested and proven, was forged between an Indian and a Rhodesian regiment, standing sponsor for Rhodesia in breadth of mind and depth of principle.

After we, as rear-guard, had marched about a quarter of a mile, information was received that a wounded man had been left on the field. Hitherto the enemy had dealt sudden death and mutilation to all falling into their hands, Red Cross or combatant; yet Capt. Ellis, our Medical Officer, on hearing of it, at once returned accompanied only by one medical orderly, to search the battlefield for that wounded man, well knowing that short shrift awaited him if the enemy had followed closely and he was discovered. Shot and shell chased our retirement, yet he moved through all, accompanied only by Medical-Orderly Gaunt, and found that the man reported wounded was already dead.

I recommended him for the first time for a decoration: on more than one occasion I had seen this unassuming hero dressing gunshot wounds under fire, gentle as a mother over her child, calm yet anxious, and muttering language surpassing that of the average medical student in volume and variation.

The casualties amongst the regiments forming the flank attack, and details in all about 3,000 strong, were 103, including 14 killed and 22 missing. Of the Rhodesia Regiment, Sergt. Carter (ex-B.S.A.P.), 1010 Pte. Puckle and 1212 Pte. Jamieson were killed; Ptes. 1296 Kemp, 1423 Van Heerden, 1171 Corpl. Boddington severely wounded; Lieut. McKenzie, 814 L.-Corpl. Stratton, Ptes. 1402 Melville, 980 Rickards, 1460 Kennedy slightly wounded.

In order to portray the battle of Salaita, it has been necessary to state that a British Brigade broke in front of an effective defence. What I have said has in no way been written in disparagement of two regiments which, having learnt their lesson here, proved their worth and their intrinsic value in many tight corners, in several well-fought combats. Training and discipline followed disorder and defeat, and fashioned of splendid material regiments fit to fight in any field. They were as those of whom Rudyard Kipling writes in the "Drums of the Fore and Aft":

> That have a black mark against their names which they will then wipe out; and it will be extremely inconvenient for the troops on whom they do their wiping. If they can be made to come again they are not pleasant men to meet; because they will not break twice.

The battle was obviously fought in order that the railway might be pushed forward, and Salaita stood in the path. Further, it was necessary to make a direct assault on the position; the one executed was well planned and conceived. It will be seen in a future chapter how General Smuts dealt with the same military situation.

The official *communiqué* published in the *Leader* at Nairobi on February 13th reads: "On the 12th instant our troops carried out a successful reconnaissance towards Salaita." This travesty needs no comment.

CHAPTER VIII.

ON February 17th the 3rd King's African Rifles marched into Serengetti. The S.A. Brigade was at Mbuyuni. On February 20th General Smuts visited Serengetti—Smuts in a British khaki uniform!

Just think of all it signified! Symbol of his personal greatness, signet of England's just rule. Soldier every inch he looked, confident, strangely immobile in face, man of a few words crisp and to the point; a thoughtful brow, eyes keen as razor-blades, and gifted with an imagination tuned to the apex of vision, that revealed to him the enemy's concentrations, their lines in the forest, their marches and their movements in country beyond the frowning hills. Imperial soldiers, perhaps, did and will discount his strategy and his " grand tactics," for he was not of the brotherhood. The Nemesis of those little printed letters (*p.s.c.*) did not follow his name in the Army List. His soldiering was learnt in a hard school, harder than Sandhurst and Camberley; in a little boys' school playing a losing game, a game played against those tutored and trained in the Art of War. How thoroughly he learnt that game and its few simple rules is shown in his faultless strategy and considered " grand tactics." If his tools were not always tempered as he trusted, and sometimes broke in his hand, how could he achieve the works his brain conceived? A soldier he stood, past-master in the red Art of War. He may not have gained the love of his mixed troops, drawn from almost every quarter of the Empire—North, East, West and South—but he won at once respect, and above all their confidence.

"An army marches on its stomach." Smuts's army of necessity, by reason of scanty communications, marched on a very lean and empty stomach, a stomach scraping its backbone.

How could the Commander be loved who forced on the hungry, the weary, and the fever-drenched; always urging onward in pursuit, urging those troops who themselves thought they had come to the length of their tether in a fever-stricken, pestilential country, in the face of a resolute enemy. Smuts brooked no excuse, took no tally, refused to realize exhaustion, and himself set an example in the indefatigable. No headquarter bureaucratic soldier he, pondering over maps and schemes; he

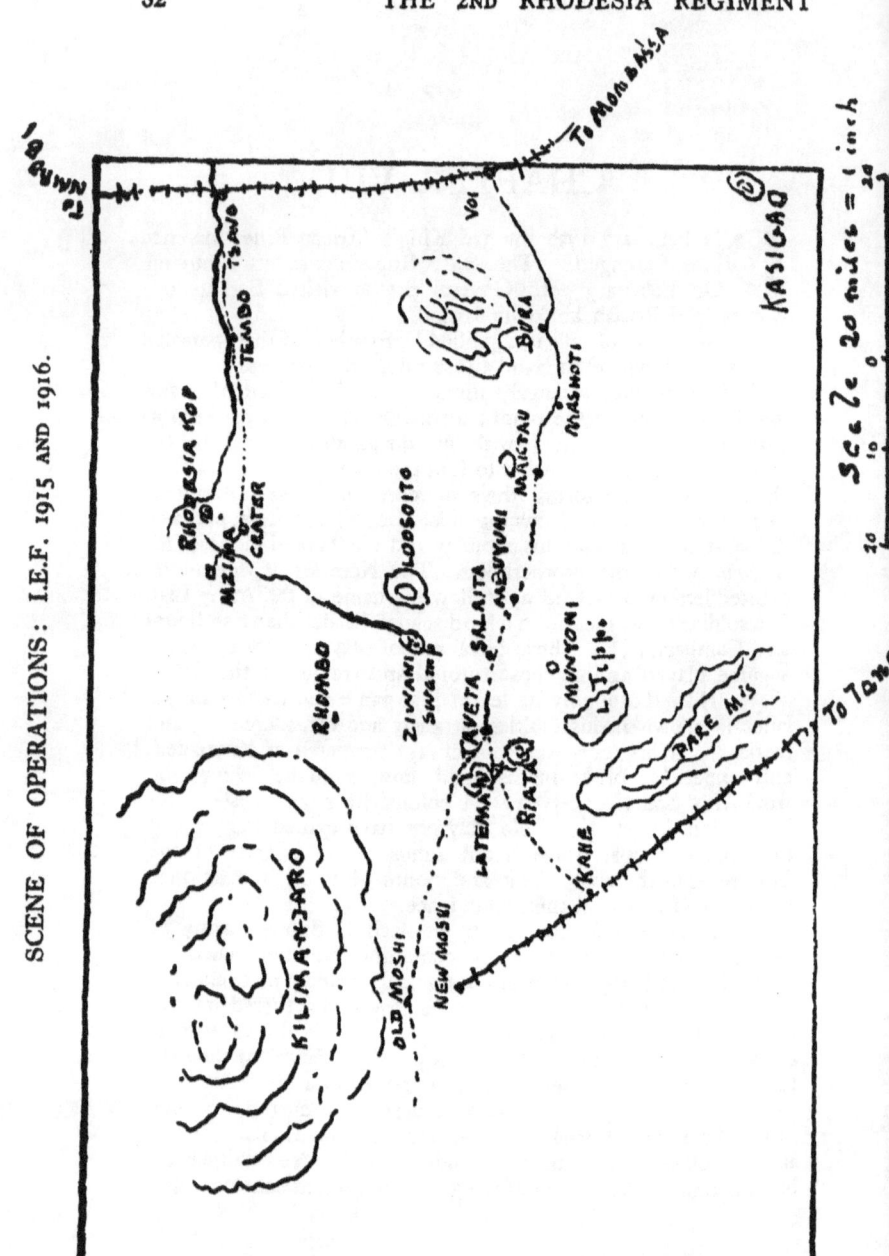

SCENE OF OPERATIONS: I.E.F. 1915 AND 1916.

sought first-hand information, near and often in the firing line, sharing the hard fare of the soldiers who served and trusted him, and if it had not been for the rations or want of them, would have loved him.

General Smuts went to the ridge beyond Ngoro spruit on February 20th, and it was commonly reported in camp that he climbed a tree there, gazed steadily at the enemy terrain for a long time, and then uttered one brief sentence: " No necessity to attack Salaita."

Intelligence of the enemy was scanty, their dispositions obscure, and it was necessary for us to pierce his outpost line; and as usual when special work was afoot, the Rhodesians were asked what they could do. Sergt. Guiney, Corpl. Ledenham, Ptes. Bayliffe, Birkett, Cowie and Andreasen undertook the hazardous venture, and gathered invaluable information; only Birkett did not return.

On the night of February 25th-26th very heavy rain fell, and three mules tied in a dug-out were drowned; and yet the troops were still on one gallon per diem of pipe-carried water. Dysentery was very prevalent in these days at Serengetti camp, and the sick report showed an average of 75 cases in the Regiment daily, and Major Cashel and Lieuts. McKenzie and Thomas go to hospital. Everyone suffered in a degree—some more, some less; it was epidemic.

On Monday, March 6th, the 2nd and 3rd S.A. Brigades march into Serengetti from Mbuyuni, and on the 7th operation orders are issued and welcomed by all after a prolonged period of inactivity, except for the almost daily little scraps indulged in by the Mobile Column detailed for the day—indecisive minor combats useful as feints and feelers, gathering information as to the enemy's dispositions and strength, keeping the mind busy and the body fit.

The orders were that the S.A. Horse, supported by the S.A.I. Brigade, would move on the night of the 7th to seize Chala, a prominent hill on the left flank of the enemy's position at Taveta; the 1st East African Brigade (ours) to " contain " Salaita on the morrow to assist the turning movement, which was the main operation. A pretty enough little scheme, and simple, except for the natural difficulties of the country.

It would be interesting to follow the S.A.H. on their night march, and to describe in detail how they seized Chala hill, and how the S.A.I. in support held the Lumi river, against a persistently attacking enemy; but if it was written here it would only be hearsay and might be inaccurate. All that can be said with certainty is that the operation was successful.

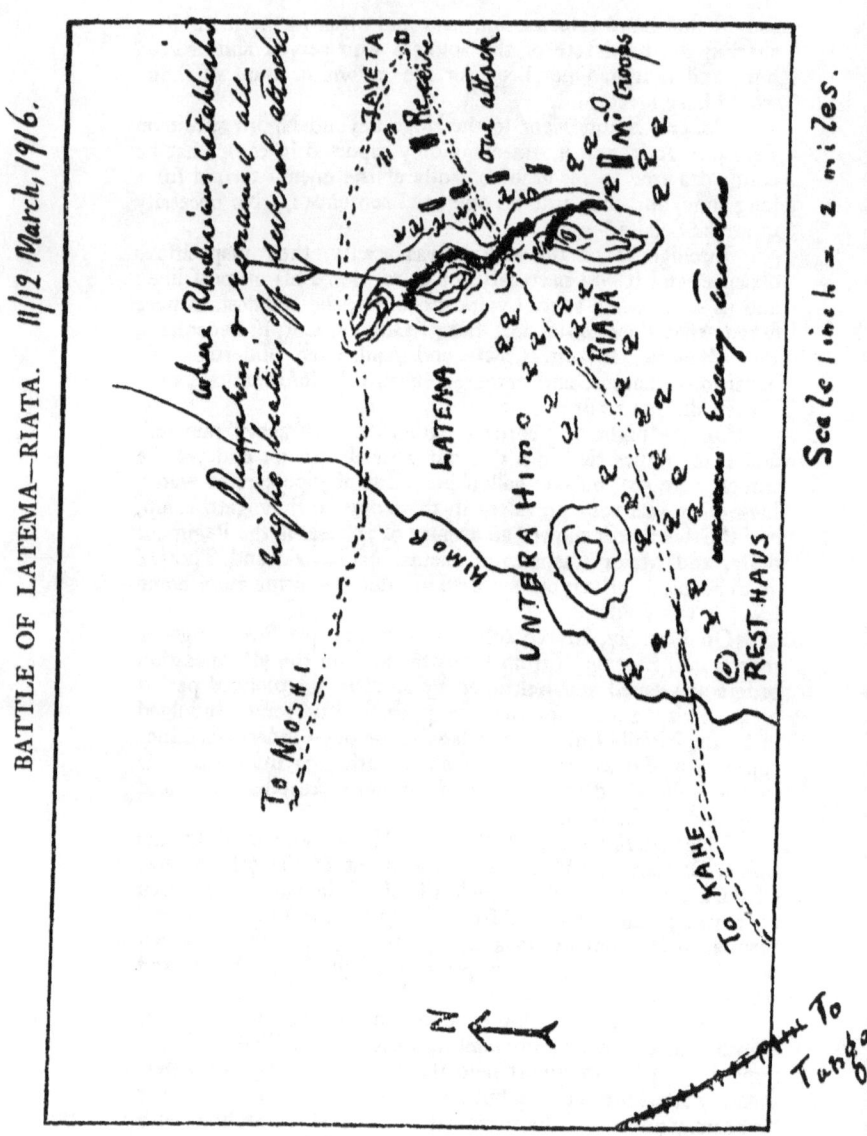

BATTLE OF LATEMA—RIATA. 11/12 March, 1916.

On the 8th the guns, supported by the 1st E.A. Brigade, bombarded Salaita from Ngoro river; and on the 9th, after another bombardment in the morning, advanced to attack the position. It was found unoccupied—Smuts's turning movement had evacuated it, without as much as a shot being fired. He had arranged for the German troops withdrawing from Salaita to Taveta to be attacked in flank during their march, but this plan miscarried. A survey of Salaita hill disclosed a position almost impregnable, honeycombed with earthworks, seamed with communication trenches, surrounded by obstacles.

On Friday, March 10th, the 1st E.A. Brigade marched for Taveta, a border village on British soil, long held by the enemy —perhaps the only hamlet of ours occupied by the Germans during the Great War. We reached the Lumi at midday, and the Regiment started on making a drift across the river in true South African style. While busily employed in this work, hasty word was brought that the enemy were re-occupying Taveta, 1½ miles west; followed a hasty scamper to arms, a flurried "fall in," and an eager pressing forward, only to find the report incorrect, and the strongly-entrenched position of Taveta unoccupied by the enemy, who were holding Latema and Riata hills and pass, 4,000 yards west.

The whole enemy position had been "turned" on March 8th by the brilliant night march to and capture of Chala hill by the South Africans. Salaita and Taveta, both strongly entrenched positions, were abandoned without an attempt at defence, without the firing of a shot; abandoned under pressure, not of volition. The enemy retired, and held Latema and Riata hills, 4,000 yards west of Taveta, and still occupied Moshi, the rail-head.

But now, and here, a tool had broken in the master worker's hand; he had deflected the Kajiado-Magadi railway to Longido, had ordered a column from there to march round the western slopes of Kilimanjaro on Moshi, synchronizing with the turning of Salaita and Taveta. The column was late, late, late, days late!—the enemy stationed at Moshi entrained there, and the remainder ejected from Latema and Riata were able to reach the rail at Kahe and entrain there.

Had that tool not failed, the operation would have been decisive; Moshi rail-head seized, Kahe occupied, the enemy entrapped, robbed of communications, short of ammunition, out-generalled and beaten. And the East African Campaign might then and there have been brought to a brilliant conclusion. Hard luck on Smuts—hard luck!

It was left for him to endeavour with immediately available

troops to drive the enemy off Latema and Riata, capture Moshi, and if possible to hold Kahe before the enemy from Latema and Riata could get there and entrain. This minor and subsidiary operation forced upon him—by defection of the Longido column—failed by minutes, and that portion of the enemy that might even then have been cut off, just escaped.

Had the column working round Kilimanajaro, from Longido to Moshi, been approximately up to time, the battle of Latema and Riata would probably never have been fought; for the enemy's position would have been so desperate that anything but a perfunctory show of resistance prior to a general surrender would have been vainglorious and futile.

But Latema and Riata was destined to be fought, and this is how it was done.

On Saturday, March 11th, about midday, the 1st E.A. Brigade moved out of Taveta to attack Latema and Riata hills, covering the road to Kahe on the German Central railway, a mere "pass" between them, which rose rugged and bush-covered some 300-400 feet above the grassy plain. The attack was preceded by a heavy bombardment of the enemy positions, to which they did not reply; then about 2 p.m. the 130th Baluchis and 3rd K.A.R. deployed to the attack, and were met by a heavy rifle, pom-pom, and machine-gun fire, and eventually were held up unable to gain fire superiority.

About 3 p.m. I requested permission for the 2nd Rhodesia Regiment to advance to " ginger up " the operation; it was rightly refused, for there were no other reserves, a fact of which at the time I was unaware. At 5 p.m., a reserve of S.A.I. was available, and the 2nd Rhodesia Regiment were ordered to advance and carry forward with them the firing line of the 130th Baluchis and 3rd K.A.R. Unhappy the time! The Regiment advanced over the open vlei country, as though on a parade ground, steadily marching on into a zone beaten by shot and shell—advanced with dazzled vision against two black hills silhouetted against the glow of the setting sun; hills in such deep shadow that choice of an aiming mark was out of the question, a sight impossible of an enemy that fired incessantly at troops crossing a sun-lit plain.

At last the shade thrown by the hills was reached, and fire was opened; but it was too late—an hour too late; the 130th Baluchis and 3rd K.A.R. were already retiring, withdrawing from a position they had held for three-and-a-half hours. To carry them forward with us to the assault was not possible, so the Rhodesians advanced alone on those two black hills, alone and unsupported except by 5 gallant British officers and 10 rank and file of the 3rd K.A.R. who pressed on with us.

Another hour of daylight and the position might even have been captured; a strong footing would certainly have been established. Coker and Dunn with " A " and " B " Companies pressed far on into the enemy stronghold, ably supported by McCarthy; but night fell, and touch was soon lost on the dark bush-clad slopes—company lost contact with company in the outer darkness, section with section, man with man. Ammunition ran out in rapid fire at point-blank ranges; the ammunition mules heavily shelled in the initial stages of the action had been ordered to cover in the bush, and could not be found, and as ammunition of units neared vanishing point, each reluctantly left the hard-won ground. Two companies in reserve held the lower slopes till well into the night, when a heavy counter-attack was delivered from three sides, an attack by an overwhelming force had it pressed on. But it was beaten off, and it then being obvious that all our forces had withdrawn and the action had been broken off, it in turn retired, with only 12 rounds per man remaining out of 300 each had taken into action.

But some of the stray and disconnected parties, separated by darkness, had individually established themselves on the crest of the enemy's position, and once there, there they remained, heavily and intermittently attacked, snatching the intervals to dress and tend their wounded; while one courageous but wild-eyed hero watched for an oncoming enemy, an enemy that came again and again out of the gloom, vanished and left its dead. Rhodesians only of the Army in East Africa kept their vigil on the heights of Latema on the night of March 11th and 12th, two isolated little clumps of men who had won through in the darkness to the summit, and refused to move therefrom.

When the moon rose at 3 a.m. two battalions of S.A.I. gallantly assaulted this prepared position; no element of surprise was present or initiated, just a night attack upon an enemy ready for it—how could it succeed? It dwindled and wilted and faded away before a merciless fire.

At daybreak reconnoitring parties crested the hills, found them unoccupied by the enemy, and occupied only by two little detached parties of Rhodesians, the only troops of five battalions that had gained and maintained a footing on them in the face of a stubborn and resolute resistance.

One hour more of daylight!—the attack of the 2nd Rhodesians launched but one hour sooner!—and the Hill Latema would have been taken by them. As it was, a splendid attempt, frustrated by darkness and shortage of ammunition, was made.

Acts of individual and collective gallantry, devotion to duty and sacrifice, were numerous, and enabled me proudly to bring to the notice of superior authority the names of the following Officers, N.C.O.'s, and men: Capt. H. O. Coker, Lieut. A. Frielinghaus, Col.-Sergt. G. Green, L.-Sergt. D. M. King, Corpls. W. H. Ballinger and Evans, Ptes. R. Ward-Smith, Needham, S. B. Jones, R. Graigh, R. H. Broembsen, F. Marney, A. B. Cooper, F. R. Trapp, C. Sheard, and N. Inskipp. And all might be referred to as falling within those immortal lines: "We could not do more, we would not do less."

Sixteen officers and 525 rank and file marched into this action and suffered sixty casualties, namely: Killed 15, missing 2, severely wounded 11, wounded 23, slightly wounded 9. The names of the killed and wounded are given in the Appendix.

On the morrow we buried our brave and splendid dead, and for each one, by the tally, we interred ten of the enemy—an enemy ousted from his stronghold by persistent and courageous if ill-timed attacks, forced to abandon guns, Maxims, ammunition, stores and equipment.

And a senior officer on the day after the fight spoke to Lieut. Reckenzaun, of the Intelligence Department, and said: "Whenever I meet a man of the 2nd Rhodesia Regiment I feel that I would like to take off my hat to him."

The Regiment was again quickly dwindling, Serengetti having proved a most unhealthy camp. Majors Cashel and Coope, Capt. Gordon, Lieuts. O. Frielinghaus, Graham, Thomas, Nicol and Stokes were already in hospital, with a proportionate number of the rank and file, and now the action at Latema-Riata put some 50 more *hors-de-combat*, so that on March 16th, "A" Company, sadly depleted, was the only one with two effective officers, and on that date Surg.-Capt. Ellis and Lieut. Allen the Quartermaster were taken to hospital.

On March 18th, I was ordered to move forward with a half battalion of 2nd Rhodesia Regiment, 130th Baluchis, 2 armoured cars, and No. 9 Field Battery, to co-operate with two battalions S.A.I. from Himo river in attacking Untera-Himo, a bald round hill rising solitary from the surrounding plain, and which the enemy, 2,000 strong, were reported to be entrenching and fortifying. I cannot think that they ever seriously intended to hold it, as in face of a fairly heavy preliminary bombardment they withdrew, leaving two dead.

On Sunday, the 19th, my column as detailed above was ordered to support the left of an attack by the 3rd South African

Brigade on Resthaus, only some eight miles distant from Untera-Himo. Unfortunately, the rear of the S.A. Brigade was thrown back and the line pierced by a vigorous enemy counter-attack, culminating in an order for the retirement to positions occupied on the previous night.

Heavy fighting was going on by day and night in the direction of Kahe, General Sheppard's Brigade being consistently engaged ; but as this portion of an extensively planned operation did not come immediately into the scope of the 2nd Rhodesia Regiment, news of events that happened came slowly to us, and may be unreliable, therefore will not be recounted. But the whole was subsidiary to and following on a great plan that had failed because the march of troops from Longido had not been coincident with the turning of Salaita and Taveta positions.

The enemy at Resthaus shelled us on the evening of March 21st at Untera-Himo, but did no damage, to speak of—just an expression of their evening " Hate."

On the 22nd, Lieut. Cowper and 23 men of the depleted half-battalion of 2nd Rhodesia Regiment I had with me left for hospital. On the same day I was ordered to attack Resthaus with the troops before mentioned and constituting my column. Our scouts got in touch with enemy picquets, but on our pressing forward an almost impregnable position was found evacuated—hot meals, porridge and stores were still in the beautifully-constructed trenches. The occupants had got out and retired hurriedly, but not I think from panic or fear ; they had simply been serving as a screen and guard for the main withdrawal which had been accomplished by the enemy. After handing over the position in the evening to the 10th Regiment S.A.I., we returned through the darkness to our camp at Untera-Himo.

On the 23rd, another 26 men are taken away in ambulances to the rear, their temperatures varying from 103 to 104 degrees.

Ah ! it was too sickening, too disheartening. These officers, these men who feared nothing on earth. Just think of it—23 of your acquaintances taken to hospital one day, 26 on the next, all carted off in ambulances, carried from your midst, from your visiting circle. Well, panic would spread ; rumours of influenza, plague and cholera would make you quake and fly to disinfectants and antidotes. It was but the daily toll from a European regiment in East Africa.

On the 25th I received orders to move the Regiment to Taveta ; 36 of the remnant of the half-battalion at Untera-Himo were unable to march, and had to be carried. The daily marches under the tropical sun, with the occasional fights, in a fever-stricken area have been too hard on those who for twelve months have worked and fought in all the work and all the fights in the most trying localities of a trying country.

Welcome orders came on the 25th that the Regiment was to move to near Nairobi for a rest ; and at 4.30 p.m. on the 27th we entrained at Taveta, 15 officers and 389 men out of a strength of 800—333 all told eventually reaching Nairobi on the 29th.

CHAPTER IX.

SMUTS now threw troops into Arusha, 50 miles west of Moshi, on the main trunk road to Kilamatinde via Kondoa-Irangi, thereby threatening the great central railway, and forcing the enemy to divide his forces for its protection.

The enemy had been pushed across the Ruwu river, abandoning a 4·1 inch *Köningsberg* gun at Kahe, and now held in force the line of the Ruwa and the Pare mountains south-east of it, a range running parallel and close to the Usambara railway almost to the coast at Tanga.

The battle of Latema and Riata, occupation of Moshi and Arusha, the sanguinary operations round Kahe and Soko Nassai, terminated a phase which, with good fortune, or to speak plainly, good workmanship, might have proved a finality.

Smuts had fruitlessly contrived all that was possible of achievement before the " great rains " broke. The god of battles ordained that his simple plans, great in their simplicity, should turn awry, and an enemy out-generalled, out-manœuvred, half-beaten, and miserably short of ammunition, should find refuge behind the swollen Ruwa river and in the Pare mountains, whilst an almost daily deluge rendered our troops immobile.

Then, at this critical time, when the enemy were in dire and threatened straits, there steamed into Sudi Bay a fair ship, a blockade runner, a vessel that had defied our Navy, crept through the line of outpost-watching war-ships, great and small, that guarded our seaboard—she dared all, accomplished all in the teeth of the mightiest Navy the world has known—off-loaded the very latest in shells and projectiles, suited for the cannon the enemy had in the field ; augmented their armament by two batteries of latest pattern 4-inch howitzers, with shells marked

OCTB (HL7 O) 1914
HL
20

and long cartridges for the 4·1 inch guns of the *Köningsberg* bearing the stamp

PATRONEN FABRIK
X O 1915
KARLSRUHE
137

and a stack of small arms, ammunition and equipment; plainly demonstrating that the ship had lately left German waters, and evaded our watchful Navy. Thus the enemy succeeded to a new lease of life, and thus a campaign, almost concluded, was prolonged till the Great Armistice was signed.

Again hard luck on Smuts: a weak spot had been found in the most dependable bit of machinery in the world—the British Navy.

The Sudi Bay ship surely off-loaded the most expensive cargo ever carried to sea; and, as far as we know, having done so, went her way unscathed, unhindered.

Major-General Sir Michael Tighe, on returning to India, sent the following farewell message from Kilindini on March 31st, 1916: " Good-bye and all good luck to the old guard: Loyal North Lancs, Rhodesians, 130th Baluchis, K.A.R., and Kashmir Rifles." Troops who had served him devotedly, and with a real respect and affection for his person and admiration for his bravery, troops that he constantly and feelingly referred to as " the old guard."

General Smuts, on taking over the command, issued the following order: " Special order, Nairobi, February 19th, 1916: On assuming command of His Majesty's forces in East Africa, I desire to express to Major-General Tighe and all ranks under his command my appreciation of the admirable work performed by the British, Indian and local forces in East Africa, often in circumstances which have made that work difficult, and have tended necessarily to restrict the scope of military operations, and especially those of an offensive nature. With better means at our disposal than it has been possible hitherto to provide with the added strength derived from reinforcements from the Union of South Africa, and by continued effort on the part of the troops which have until now borne the burden of the local campaign, I feel assured that success of a substantial nature will attend the operations which will be undertaken with the object of defeating the enemy in the field. To this end, a whole-hearted co-operation of all ranks and all units is indispensable, and on that co-operation I rely with confidence."

Brigadier-General Sheppard assumed command of the 1st East African Brigade, resting and training at Mbuyuni, less the 2nd Rhodesia Regiment at Kabete, a command he held until the time the Rhodesians left East Africa. It may be said of this Commander that he enlisted and held the affection of every man under his command—a command composed of many races, inclining to many creeds: British, Indian, African, Christian, Mahomedan, Pagan. His ready smile, a note of cheerfulness and fair play, found response on the faces of enigmatic Asiatics, impassive Africans, and resolute Europeans. Askaris, troopers, Sepoys, privates, subalterns and senior officers welcomed his appearance in their lines. A fighting General, willing to take and share risks, but not foolhardy hazards. His bible was Part I. of Field Service Regulations, and he carried it in his pocket; his creed: "I believe in the British and Indian Army; in encountering the enemy on all occasions; in beating him if I can; and if I can't making the best I can of the situation, and being cheerful under all and any circumstances." No wonder he was beloved of his Brigade—soldier, sportsman, optimist, fighter, and philosopher.

Chaplain-Capt. Dennis Jones joined us at Kabete; he came from the Mediterranean Command, and bore traces of the hard Gallipoli campaign; he became in time a favourite with all ranks.

Lieut. Brett-Young, R.A.M.C., also joined us here to relieve Capt. Ellis who was granted seven days' leave to recuperate at Nairobi.

Several battalions of King's African Rifles were being formed at this time, and difficulty was found in getting suitable men to officer them. Although we could ill spare of our best, I was constrained by the urgency of the appeal and the exigencies of the service to permit Capt. Dunn, Lieut. Mitchell, Sergt. Brown, Corpls. Catchpole, Huggins, and Davies, Ptes. Evans, Woods and Hamling to transfer to them; and one and all did excellently well in their new regiments.

Our period of rest and recuperation terminated on May 15th, 1916, when we entrained for Taveta at 6.15 p.m.—495 all ranks —reaching our destination at daylight on the 17th, where the remainder of the 1st E.A. Brigade joined us from Mbuyuni on the 19th.

On the 20th a long, long march commenced—a march down

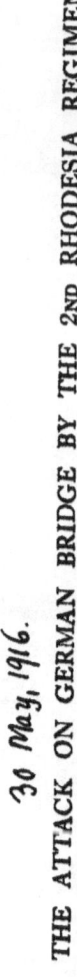

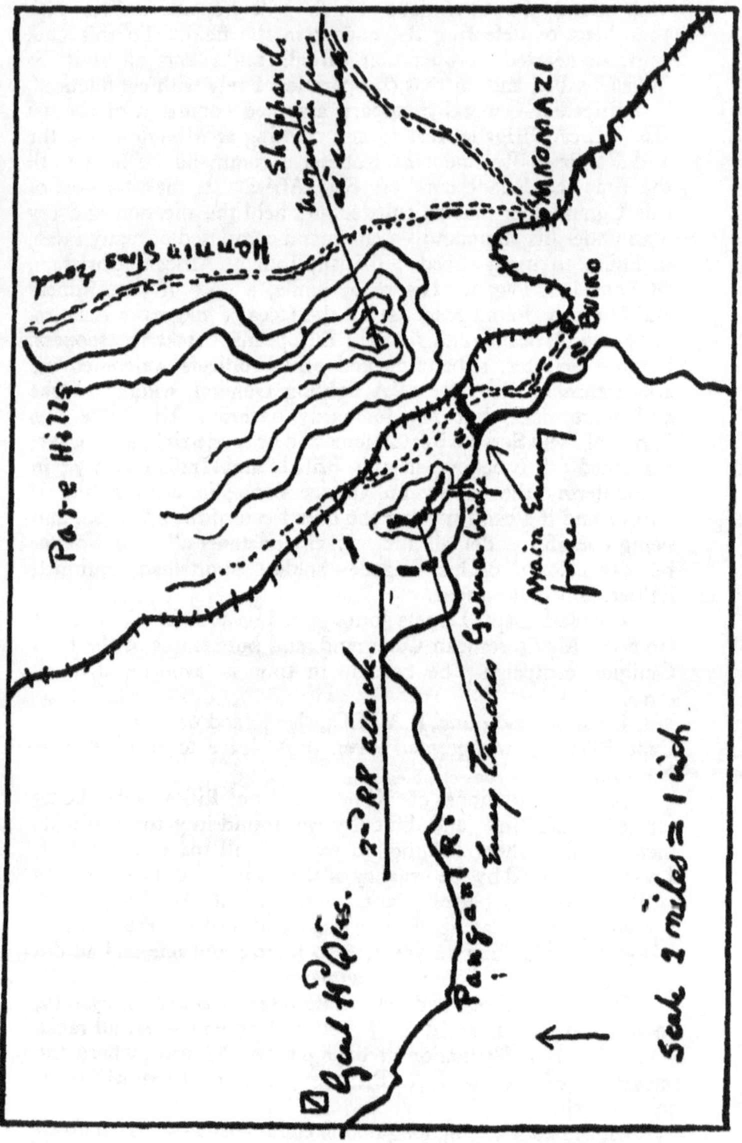

THE ATTACK ON GERMAN BRIDGE BY THE 2ND RHODESIA REGIMENT.

30 May, 1916.

the left bank of the Pangani river, a trudge through alternate sand and slough, by night and by day, and always in the deadly heat of the steaming low veldt. The 495 men who left Kabete were far from being really fit; sodden with fever, weak from prolonged dysentery, they fell out reluctantly one by one. Capt. Gordon went down on the 19th, Major Cashel was taken back on the 22nd, the ambulances were packed with men whose endurance, long tested to the utmost, collapsed suddenly, leaving mere wrecks. Two extracts from my diary will disclose the nature of the march: "Monday, May 22nd, 11.30 p.m.: Started night march, which took us till 11.30 a.m. on the 23rd, when we reached 695 on map GBE."

"Wednesday, 24th: Reached 'Rapids' at mid-day; after an hour's halt, started cutting road through bush; very hard day; got through to Pangani river about 11 p.m., without food, blankets or anything. Mules and horses stampeded at night, great commotion, everyone thought it was a night attack, fortunately no one fired a shot. Probable cause—lions."

The Pangani ran broad and swift and deep on our immediate right, but bathing was out of the question as a rather laconic entry in my diary of the 26th denotes: "Crocs. ate two South Africans and three natives to-day."

On the evening of Monday, 29th, as we marched to an unnamed point a little south-east of Kwalokua and about seven miles from the railway, the enemy opened fire on our transport and reserves with long range artillery, and shelled us pretty freely after pitching camp, until nightfall; little damage, however, was sustained.

It is necessary here to refer again to the main military situation as far as it concerned the immediate operations in which the 2nd Rhodesia Regiment participated.

The middle of May saw the enemy still holding the banks of the Ruwa river, the Pare hills, and certain stations, Same and Lembeni on the Usambara railway. About the same time of our commencing the march down the left bank of the Pangani, keeping the railway on our left and about 15 miles distant, Hannington's Brigade left Umbuyuni to turn the Pare hills and make good the line of rail. Thus it will be seen that two columns worked on more or less parallel lines some 30 miles apart with the railway midway between them, ultimately converging on Buiko on the Usambara railway. About six miles from Buiko a narrow strip or neck of bush-covered plain divides the Pare mountains and the Pangani, a pre-eminently strong position. It was from this point and from Buiko that the enemy had shelled us on the night of May 29th,

D

Smuts had foreseen the stand that would be made here, and had discounted it by sending Hannington's Brigade round the eastern slopes of the Pare mountains to debouch from the Pass at Buiko on the enemy's right flank and rear, whilst we attacked the enemy entrenched in the narrow neck before referred to. An admirably planned and simple scheme, involving a march of 150 miles to a culminating point.

The enemy had withdrawn before Hannington's Brigade, contesting several positions on the line of rail, till, on the 29th, they were concentrated in the vicinity of Buiko, and strongly holding the strip between Pangani river and Pare mountains. The completeness in plan of Smuts's " grand tactics " is again in evidence ; the parallel columns were individually strong enough to look after themselves, therefore had the enemy commander elected to stand against Hannington and force a decision, the 1st Division, of which the 1st East African Brigade formed a part, might easily have been thrown across his communications near Buiko. The withdrawal was imposed upon him ; he chose to make a stand on the strip that divides the Pangani river and Pare mountains, but Smuts's march had been so unexpectedly rapid and his tactics so forceful that he found himself in that vicinity before the completion of the strategical bridge across the Pangani, on which the strength of the position was based. His defence of it was far from whole-hearted, and it only required moderate pressure to induce him to continue his retirement along the line of rail. I am not in a position to say whether Hannington's column was behind scheduled time in its arrival at Mkomazi near Buiko, but to the ordinary onlooker a closer co-operation appeared to have been possible and advantageous.

But to return to regimental concerns. Daylight on May 30th witnessed the Rhodesians marching out from the over-night bivouac towards the enemy position. It was being given something to do individually, unsupported, unassisted. It moved cheerfully to its task—now but 300 strong and indomitable men, men who had fought and conquered disease, scorned fatigue, and had seen and kept " duty " before them as a lodestar. It marched towards an entrenched position sited at a bend in the Pangani, between river and rail, against the enemy's front line, guarding a strategic bridge three-quarters finished across the broad waters : a bridge under construction to aid a possible retirement from the position we assaulted, or from the Pare mountains, if communications were cut at Buiko, or for the purpose of launching troops against the right flank of an attacking force. As the Regiment came within effective range, it was met

IN EAST AFRICA 67

by a heavy but ill-directed rifle fire; the Regiment, already deployed, advanced in a spectacular fashion, as though executing a field firing exercise near the long range in Salisbury, section supporting section, covered by machine-gun fire. Rapidly it pressed forward to within 200 yards, gaining superiority of fire gradually but surely; never wavering in the face of an enemy of approximately equal strength holding a scientifically-entrenched position. At 200 yards the enemy company must have felt the game was lost, must have realized his resolute assailants meant to press home to the last arbitrament of the bayonet; for with an accord, or by order, Askaris leapt from their entrenchments, momentarily offering such a target that machine-gunners dream of: rifle and Maxim fire exacted a heavy toll ere they disappeared into the falling ground behind the position. Many fights have I witnessed, but never before have I seen " Infantry Training " and " Field Service Regulations " entirely and completely vindicated; never before seen the use of every scrap of natural cover minimizing casualties, and falsifying the enemy's aim; never seen machine-guns working round the flanks surely and surreptitiously between bursts of fire, one covering the other; never witnessed before in action the results of perfect fire control and fire discipline. As a consequence of properly applied drill-book tactics an enemy of approximately equal strength was driven from a prepared and entrenched position, in disorder and rapid retreat, having only inflicted the following casualties on us: Killed, No. 10 Native Scout Levi; dangerously wounded, 773 Sergt. T. G. Addicott, 685 Sergt. C. G. Wood; seriously wounded, Lieut. Nicol, 1172 L.-Corpl. Ballam, 1451 Pte. L. Rothstein; wounded, Capt. A. L. Tribe, 1075 L.-Corpl. J. T. Marshall, 1181 Pte. E. F. Burdett, 1403 Pte. H. F. Mackintosh, 730 Pte. C. Cock.

The position was at once held and consolidated, and a donga in advance of it was occupied and improved. A feeble counter-attack was driven off, and the enemy satisfied himself with sniping until evening, when he opened a considerable shell fire on his erstwhile encampment, but most of the projectiles passed harmlessly overhead and burst in the bush a hundred yards out of bounds.

General Sheppard had in the morning started with an Indian regiment and a battery of mountain guns to scale the difficult Pare hills; by dusk he had reached a point overlooking German bridge, as the scene of the recent conflict was called, and witnessed a close marshalling of enemy troops, preparatory to launching a strong counter-attack with the object of retaking their lost position. A splendid target was afforded—a target such as a gunner's fancy paints in moments of reverie but seldom offers itself in reality. The little mountain-guns barked and belched from their giddy pinnacles, scattering formations and breaking up the concentration. Once more the enemy must have realized the game was lost.

During the morning the 29th Punjabis had been sent up in support, but were not used until nightfall, when they were placed on perimeter duty.

The next day, May 31st, the advance was continued, the Rhodesians again leading, but I had been given the 25th Royal Fusiliers, 29th Punjabis, and 5th South African Infantry as well. The enemy retired without offering opposition, and we occupied Buiko, which they shelled with a 4·1 inch gun in the evening, inflicting little if any damage.

The action at German bridge had cost the enemy many lives—8 dead Askari were found in the position, and 19 in the vicinity.

I had great pleasure in bringing to the notice of superior authority the names of Capt. Blagrove and Lieut. Hare for bravery and good leadership.

CHAPTER X.

FROM Thursday, June 1st, till Tuesday, the 6th, the troops rested at Buiko, after a march of 150 miles accomplished in ten days. Fifteen miles daily sounds little enough, but it included fighting, cutting roads, and perpetual reconnaissance in unknown trackless country; and it was the march of a Division encumbered with mixed transport, not a small column or patrol in light marching order.

At 4.30 a.m. on the 6th the Regiment, acting as advance-guard, crossed to the right bank of the Pangani river by a bridge of Berthon boats; several animals went over the side into the deep swift water, but all were rescued. The 29th Punjabis had gone ahead road-making, and were camped at Kitumbatu. As we were halted at Palms, some eight miles from Buiko, a report came in that the enemy were advancing in force on both sides of the Pangani; so our march was resumed with the intention of reinforcing the 29th Punjabis, but on reaching their camp it was ascertained that the rumour was based on unreliable native intelligence, and that only small enemy patrols had been observed.

The 7th and 8th were devoted to a very hard road-making task, and on the latter date " A " and " F " Companies, who had been left at Buiko as protection to G.H.Q., rejoined.

On June 9th the Regiment marched as advance-guard to the Brigade, the 130th Baluchis and 29th Punjabis having preceded it as an independent column, entrusted principally with the duty of reconnaissance, for the terrain had become less known and even more difficult than heretofore, and a way had to be groped for. The locality sought was Makalamo, where a trolley line said to be running from Mombo to Handeni was supposed to cross the Pangani. Intelligence was scanty and unreliable, the country blanketed in almost inpenetrable bush. After about four hours marching a heavy engagement was heard in progress immediately to our front; it turned out to be the advanced column held up by a strong enemy force. The Rhodesians and 2nd Kashmir Rifles were moved up in support, but did not become engaged till two companies of the former

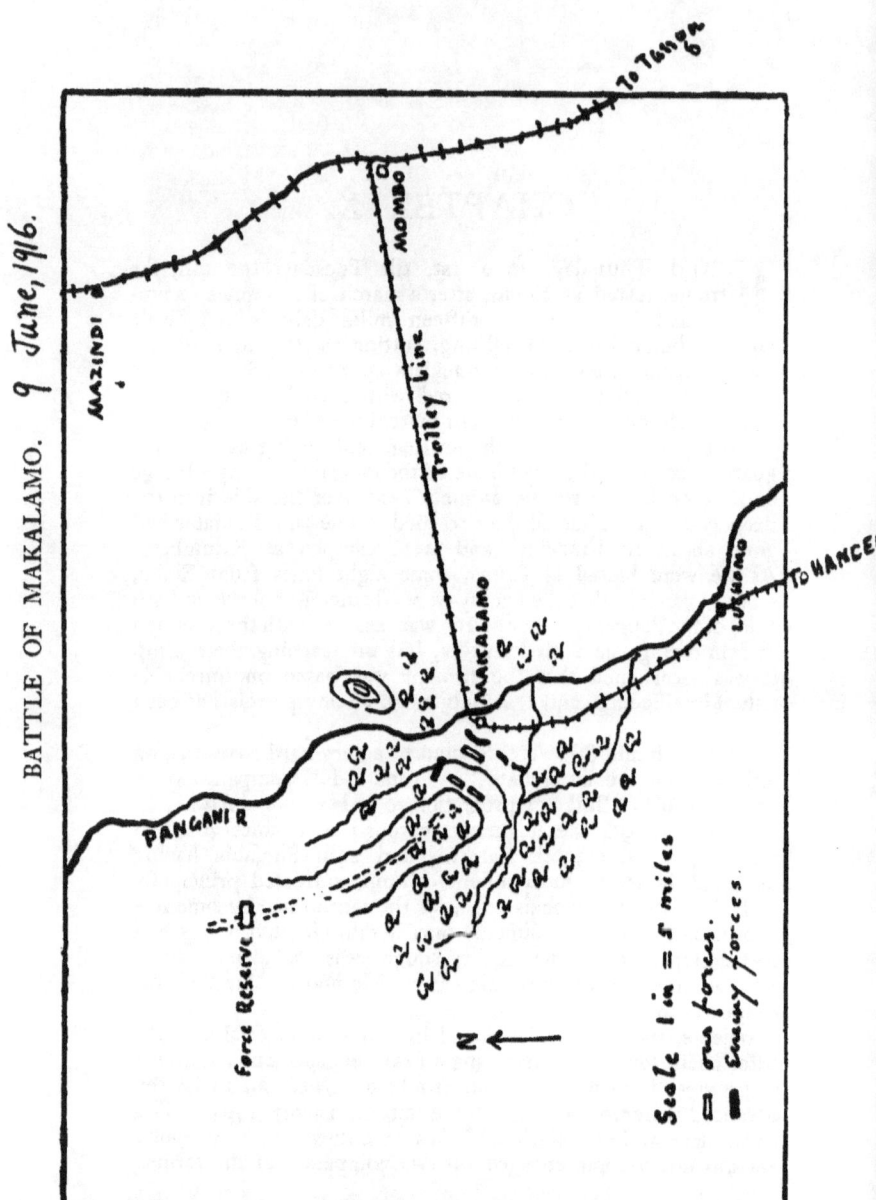

were sent about 5 p.m. to assist the withdrawal of the 130th Baluchis, who had borne the brunt of the fighting and suffered somewhat heavily.

About 3 p.m. the enemy delivered a heavy counter-attack on the supports, but it was practically ineffectual. It served only to pin to the ground those troops who were in far too close a formation to manœuvre or use their arms to any advantage; the bush was so thick that aimed fire was out of the question, and the bulk of it was very high and did little damage—the bullets zipped and hummed about five feet in the air, and the leaves fluttered to the ground thickly as in an autumn squall. Another counter-attack was made at 5.30, but proved abortive,

It was difficult for the onlooker to form a just appreciation of and to criticise the action, as he was equally befogged by the lack of information as the responsible Brigadier was by he shortage of intelligence. Napoleon has bequeathed a truism to the effect that "a general who is ignorant of his enemy's strength and dispositions, is ignorant of his trade"; but Napoleon never fought in the dense bush and forest of Eastern Africa. Troops there might as well have been participating in continual night operations, for touch and information often could only be gained and maintained at fifty yards distance and at the muzzle of a rifle; cohesion could as easily be lost irretrievably by units diverging fifty yards from the line of direction. Almost the whole campaign might be likened to a huge night operation, a groping in the obscurity of Darkened Africa.

Thus it was not positively assured that there was any trolley-line at all between Mombo and Handeni; if there was, it was uncertain where it crossed the Pangani. In point of fact, Smuts with that almost uncanny foresight and intuition before referred to, had allocated the exact spot—Makalamo— and further had timed to a minute the moment that the enemy should be crossing it, and had sent the 1st East African Brigade as it were to a trysting-place.

Wrapped in a complete ignorance of the surrounding bush-clad terrain, in dim uncertainty the fight was engaged in, uncertainty as to locality, as to what, and who, our troops had to encounter, Major Pretorious, that matchless scout, had individually done wonders, but a single scout working alone in the blackness of night, or in the utter oblivion of a bush-enshrouded country, cannot obtain much information useful to a general moving a big force; he could only reveal what he saw fifty yards away from the line he made or the track he followed— for the rest, darkness and an unopened volume.

Thus it is probable that the General Officer Commanding the immediate operation was unacquainted with the fact that we had struck the trolley-line where it crossed the Pangani at the very moment the enemy forces, turned out of the Pare mountains by Hannington's Brigade, were attempting a passage and a retreat to Handeni; and with the fact that a thousand yards distant the trolley-line crossed by a fragile bridge a deep donga, a point vulnerable in every respect, which, had he seized, would have cut the enemy off from their line of retirement to Handeni, and have pinned them to the vicinity of Makalamo, until, with the reserves available, an overwhelming force could have been launched against them. As it was, the enemy were engaged throughout the day in an indecisive action, which was broken off by us at dusk; when a great silence enveloped our camp, a silence that falls upon those who are by night in the face of the enemy, foodless, waterless, blanketless and weary, and only too ready to leave the rest till to-morrow. During the night that followed the enemy must have striven with feverish energy to clear the whole of his force and guns by use of the trolley-line, for at daybreak our patrols found but the empty workshops, shell-torn huts and houses of Makalamo, a few dead Askari, and some newly-filled graves. The enemy had disappeared in the darkness from under our very noses, and was well on his way to Handeni, tearing up with frantic fingers the trolley-line behind him.

Had one of the two regiments held in reserve been ordered on reconnaissance duty more might have been revealed as to the locality, the weak and the strong points. But there would have been a great risk to run in ordering such a line of action; for the enemy force comprising the whole Usambara command probably far outnumbered our weak brigade, and possessed intimate knowledge of the field of battle, knowledge of immeasurable value in such difficult country. The general reserve was, I believe, so far in rear that it could not have given material and early support in the event of things going wrong; in fact, the narrow road cut through the bush was already blocked by the long strung-out transport of the brigade in action. On the face of it, it seems regrettable that more was not made out of the difficult and even precarious position into which the enemy had been forced and hurried; but it would require the fullest knowledge of all the surrounding and contingent circumstances to enable any one to say if more could have been achieved than harrying the enemy and inflicting considerable loss on him in his retirement; this was done.

The regiment had not been heavily engaged, so our casualties were light : Killed, No. 920 Pte. Doyle ; wounded, 917 Corpl. Smith, 931 Pte. Lyons, 814 L.-Corpl. Stratton.

Total casualties comprised 41 killed and wounded. I had pleasure in bringing to the notice of superior authority the name of Sergt. Cranswick, 2nd Rhodesia Regiment.

On the evening of the day we entered Makalamo the 2nd Rhodesia Regiment, together with a squadron of 17th Indian Cavalry, marched out some five miles to Massini, and on the following day, strengthened by a section of the 27th Mountain Battery, formed the advance-guard to the 1st E.A. Brigade, marching on Luchomo. A mile north of Luchomo we met with some enemy resistance, which was soon brushed aside, with slight casualties on either side, Lieut. Knowles of the 17th Cavalry being killed, and two enemy Askari killed. The party of the enemy that engaged us was probably a destruction gang left behind to tear up the trolley-line, which work was very thoroughly put through ; derelict trolleys there were, but all the axle boxes were smashed.

From June 12th to 16th we pursued a retiring enemy, but with little hope of overtaking him, for his trolley-line was n good working order, and leant itself to a rapid movement of troops. It was an almost waterless march : on the first day out we sent the animals back to Luchomo to water ; on the second, we did without ; on the third, the Mbagui water-holes provided a slimy substitute. The enemy we calculated to be twelve hours ahead of us throughout, and he contented himself with desultory sniping from a skeleton rear-guard formation, a rifle-shot from a tree here and there, a crumpled man dropping inertly in the marching ranks now and then—the hand of man, an aimed rifle, guided by the hand of fate, fate that chooses which one of the moving mass of men the bullet shall find its billet in. Kismet! That was all—just sufficient to maintain that constant ever-present nerviness incidental to the whole campaign.

On June 16th we camped at Nguguini, about four miles north of Handeni, which the enemy held in force. Immediate attack was impossible, for our advance had been a long-drawn-out straggling crawl along the narrow trolley way cut through the thicket ; water sufficient only for small numbers at one time, where there was any at all.

On the 18th the Rhodesians marched, in their accustomed position as advance-guard, upon Handeni ; they paraded but 170 rifles and 6 machine-guns, out of a strength of 800—the climate and the campaign had claimed the rest. Handeni had been evacuated in the night, and the German flag no longer flung proudly from the citadel.

Handeni, a considerable village, fell into our hands, houses and huts intact, military material destroyed; enemy sick and wounded left trustfully in our keeping, typifying the faith even an enemy—hitherto somewhat unscrupulous, and only recently acknowledging and practising the chivalry of war—placed in the humanity and magnanimity of our troops. Fools we may have been at times to tend German prisoners, sick and wounded, better than we served our own comrades and men; yet foolish as it may have been, the trait is as permanent as history, and on such weak—or perhaps strong and imperishable—basis, born of a great compassion, established in the strength that helps the weak, has the great British Empire been silently built. I have seen soldiers lend blankets of which they were themselves sorely in need to German prisoners; to men who an hour before had been anxious and willing by any means, fair or foul, to take their lives. That is simply British sentiment—maudlin, foolish, weak perhaps, but ages old, and the Empire is founded on such stuff, strong in its merciful weakness.

Beves's S.A. Brigade harried the rear of the enemy retiring from Handeni and did some useful work near Pongwe, inflicting severe loss. The 5th S.A. Infantry ran into an ambush at Kangata and put up a fine fight in an indecisive engagement.

On June 23rd the 1st East African Brigade marched through Kangata to Mzinga; the former halting-place being memorable by reason of several swarms of bees, disturbed in their bark hives slung high in the timber, attacking the encroaching troops, causing disorder, commotion and much pain. I witnessed a plucky action in this connection on the part of a Rhodesian, who, accepting the "white man's burden," wrapped his blanket round a rifleman of the 3rd Kashmir Rifles, who was literally covered with bees, the while he himself was being terribly stung; the little Gurkha soldier was done to death. The heroic act seemed abortive and in vain, but perhaps it forged just one more link between East and West, another little tie between a European and a Native regiment, a regiment that we had marched with and fought beside in many places, and counted as our close friends and comrades.

The ever-welcome figure of Smuts was seen at Mzinga—goodness knows where it had blown in from, but you may depend it was from some other scene of action, within his wide theatre of war; he always seemed to be there or thereabouts when things were happening, and on this occasion he proved no faithless harbinger.

The enemy, probably a strong rear-guard, were in position on the Lukigura river, and the operation planned for his discomfiture opened at daybreak on Saturday, June 24th, by General Hoskins—with a force consisting of 2nd Kashmir Rifles, S.A. Infantry, and 25th Royal Fusiliers—being detached to our right flank to march down the Lukigura upon the enemy's left; the attack to be opened in front by the 1st East African Brigade as soon as Hoskins's action developed.

The 1st East African Brigade left their bivouac at Mzinga at 3.30 a.m., and immediately snipers began their dirty work. Willoughby's heavy armoured cars trundled along with the vanguard, and soon ran into a prepared position astride and flanking the road, from which a pom-pom opened and pierced the radiator of the leading car, causing its withdrawal amidst rifle fire. A sowar of the 17th Cavalry wandering down the road in an aimless fashion was shot, and the enemy ambush of 1 company, 1 pom-pom, and 2 Maxims retired on to its main body at Lukigura.

About 10 a.m., General Hoskins's force, after performing an arduous march through thick bush, became engaged with the enemy's left flank. Three companies 130th Baluchis, and 29th Punjabis, were pushed forward to envelop the enemy's right. The whole movement was successfully carried out, and the enemy were practically surrounded, but made a fine stand till about 4 p.m., when, under pressure from the gallant troops with General Hoskins, they broke up and essayed to escape through the cordon—melting away into the thick bush, blundering into the arms of our troops, fighting, surrendering, running; many winning to safety. Our casualties totalled only about 20, whilst we buried 4 Europeans, 20 Askari, and took 14 Europeans and many Askari prisoners.

The 2nd Rhodesia Regiment, aching to join in the brilliant little action, were held in reserve, together with three companies of the 130th Baluchis and 5th S.A.F.A.

A captured officer here informed us that Ptes. Mossop and Homan, missing after Latema, were in the enemy's hands—Mossop wounded, but doing well; also Pte. Cowie, missing after an action before Taveta, as being a prisoner of war. Sergts. Robertson and Prew appear in orders as Lieutenants vice Stokes and Usher.

The enemy shelled our camp merrily from a long range, from 5 p.m. to 8 p.m., after the fight, but did little damage.

On Tuesday, June 27th, General Sheppard pushed forward ten miles to Msiha or Makindu—or " Shell Camp," as it subsequently became known—with the 130th Baluchis and 2nd Kashmir Rifles. Snipers got very busy about this time on the road between Lukigura and Msiha and on our communications with Handeni, and many casualties occurred, including Capt. Mulligan as he travelled by car beside General Hoskins, the General Officer Commanding 1st Division. Deep trenches would be dug and covered with brushwood, sand, leaves and spoor to catch the Mechanical Transport; thin wires at bends in the road would stretch from tree to tree to fling the motor-cyclist despatch-rider from his machine. When success attended these plans, the onlooking enemy would rush out, plunder and burn the car, or capture the cyclist.

Major Cashel again went to hospital, and to our loss he did not again rejoin the Regiment but did valuable work on the Lines of Communication, work more suited to his then state of health.

CHAPTER XI.

IT was not until July 7th we left Lukigura to rejoin the 1st East African Brigade at Makindu or Msiha, where the enemy welcomed our arrival with a couple of hours bombardment. Thirty-five recruits arrived at the same time from Rhodesia, a real good lot, destined to complete their training under shell-fire.

Day now followed day monotonously, as we tarried for Smuts's far-embracing scheme to develop elsewhere. We were a division in a cramped camp, entrenched and dug in, with no guns capable of replying to those of the enemy that shelled us by day and by night, reducing to a fine art a system of annoyance and disquietude, produced by intermittent and well-timed shell-fire—say, ten shells sent over at lunch-time, four dispatched at 2 p.m. when men were resting, fifty from 4 to 6 p.m. when animals must water and preparations for the night-watch be made, two at " lights out," ten at midnight, and when at last a sound sleep was anticipated twenty-five or so would be pitched over at erratic intervals between 2 and 5 a.m.

The Rhodesians had seen over-many ineffectual projectiles launched and exploded, and were inclined to despise and belittle German shell-fire, until on the evening of July 10th No. 1496 Pte. Taylor, officers' mess caterer, who was sitting on the ground beside the mess-table, in the open—at which officers partook solemnly of the one-course dinner, bully and biscuit, and half rations at that—gave a little cry, a guttural throaty squeal, attracting the notice of Ellis, our medical officer, who first leaned from his seat, then quickly rose and turned a limp form over, to disclose the dark-red ragged-edged blot on the absorbent khaki shirt. That jagged fragment of high-explosive, burst overhead and laughed at, had accomplished its deadly errand.

So from July 7th till August 7th we endured this bombardment, daily and reluctantly making our dug-outs a little bit deeper. No one would have minded it if a deep-throated piece of ordnance of ours had spoken in reply, but our short-range guns said nothing, silently biding their time. So we simply walked, sat, and slept a little, under a considered plan of shell-fire planned to annoy us, and it annoyed ; schemed to inflict casualties and inflicting them daily, one here, one there, sometimes a little group. The distant boom of guns, and a flickering glow in the sky by night, continually presaged the drone, then the screech, and finally the ear-splitting explosion ; and men turned over, cursed our present impotency and waited, speculating upon the next to come.

The yellow spectres of fever and dysentery stalked through the sweltering sweating camp, entered the dug-outs and beckoned to their victims to come to the crowded shell-rent hospital tents ; in due time to be evacuated in motor ambulances, to be sniped or mined on their progress to the rear. In spite of incinerators that seemed capable of cremating anything, and well-thought-out and applied sanitation, the water became polluted. Animals died by scores from tsetse fly ; the whole camp was a hotbed of disease, accentuated and predisposed by reason of an inevitable depression attributable to inertia, inaction and long waiting. No letter had reached us since leaving Kahe ; no room for mail bags on those crowded cars toiling through the dust of our long but narrow communications, strenuously endeavouring to bring half-rations to the hungry and emaciated. So withal men spent much time picking small grey lice with a transparent line down the back from the seams of their seedy, threadbare khaki shirts—shirts in such a state that some would not stand washing, lest they should fall to pieces. Men who essayed to wash their clothes stood by in their overcoats whilst their only rags dried in the sun. I sent Lieut. Prew back to get kit, but he went to hospital at Mbuyuni. I despatched Lieut. H. O. Frielinghaus for stores ; he went to hospital at Taveta. Our padre, Dennis Jones, leaves us, and Chaplain-Lieut. Devenish is appointed in his place. Capt. Coker is promoted to Temporary Major, vice Major Jesser-Coope, long since sent to the rear in broken health.

At this juncture the general position must again come under consideration. The enemy force, pressed from the Usambara railway and Pare mountains, had retired before us through Handeni on to the main body of the enemy guarding Morogoro and the Central railway. Our advance had left Handeni and Lukigura in rear, but was held up at Msiha, with the enemy occupying in force a position of unusual strength, and long since prepared for defence, some nine miles ahead on the rugged slopes of Ruhungu.

The enemy force at Ruhungu to our immediate front was stronger than the force Smuts could feed even on half-rations by our precarious and narrow Line of Communications, stretching back via the Usambara railway, Taveta, Voi, to Mombasa.

The problem presented was : " How can a force in position at Msiha defeat an enemy of equal or greater strength nine miles distant, ensconced in a prepared position of unusual security on the road to Morogoro, the commercial capital on the Central railway ? No support or reinforcements can be expected, as the road will carry barely sufficient food and munitions for

IN EAST AFRICA

the troops at Msiha. The objective being the defeat of the enemy lying in the way, the occupation of Morogoro, and seizure of the great central line of rail connecting Dar-es-Salaam with the Lakes."

Smuts answered this problem by advancing Van de Venters's force to Kondoa-Irangi, threatening the Central railway at Kilamatinde. Thus the German commander was compelled to split or divide his army, one portion to " contain " Kondoa-Irangi, the other to oppose the advance via Handeni and Msiha. His force divided as Smuts contrived, either British force was able to cope with the possible opposition in front of it, as was demonstrated by the brilliant repulse by Van de Venter of a heavy and determined attack by the enemy, and by the enforced retirement of the enemy from Ruhungu and the Nguru mountains.

It is useless for anyone to belittle the forethought and military science which established this strategy in the days long ago when Taveta, Moshi, and Arusha were occupied; little events, long marches, many encounters, had led up to the present culminating point, a time when the enemy was divided into two camps far removed from each other, but in face of two British forces able to impose their will on either by force of arms. The enemy had no choice, there was no way out, no loophole left; attacks on our communications failed to prevent prosecution of Smuts's considered plan. His position was precarious: if he retained all his army at Ruhungu, Van de Venter would march to Kilimatinde and thence by the Central railway to Morogoro and place himself athwart the Lines of Communication of the German force at Ruhungu, which would then have an army in front of it and an army in rear. If he surrendered Ruhungu and opposed Van de Venter, the troops at Msiha had simply to march on the Central railway at Morogoro. He retired both camps simultaneously, his only safe plan.

Thus Smuts divided the enemy's forces, and imposed his will upon them; and it will be shown—as far as it concerns the enemy at Ruhungu, immediately in opposition to the 1st Division, which included the 1st East African Brigade—that he further planned to encompass their destruction and effect practical annihilation; but another tool broke in the master-builder's hand.

The immediate plan of action was disclosed on Sunday, August 6th. The intention of the G.O.C.-in-Chief was to clear the Nguru hills of the enemy, who held positions at Ruhungu and Kanga, with their flanks strongly protected by forces at Mahasi and Massimbani, with reserves at Turiani.

General Britz's mounted brigade was to move from Luki-

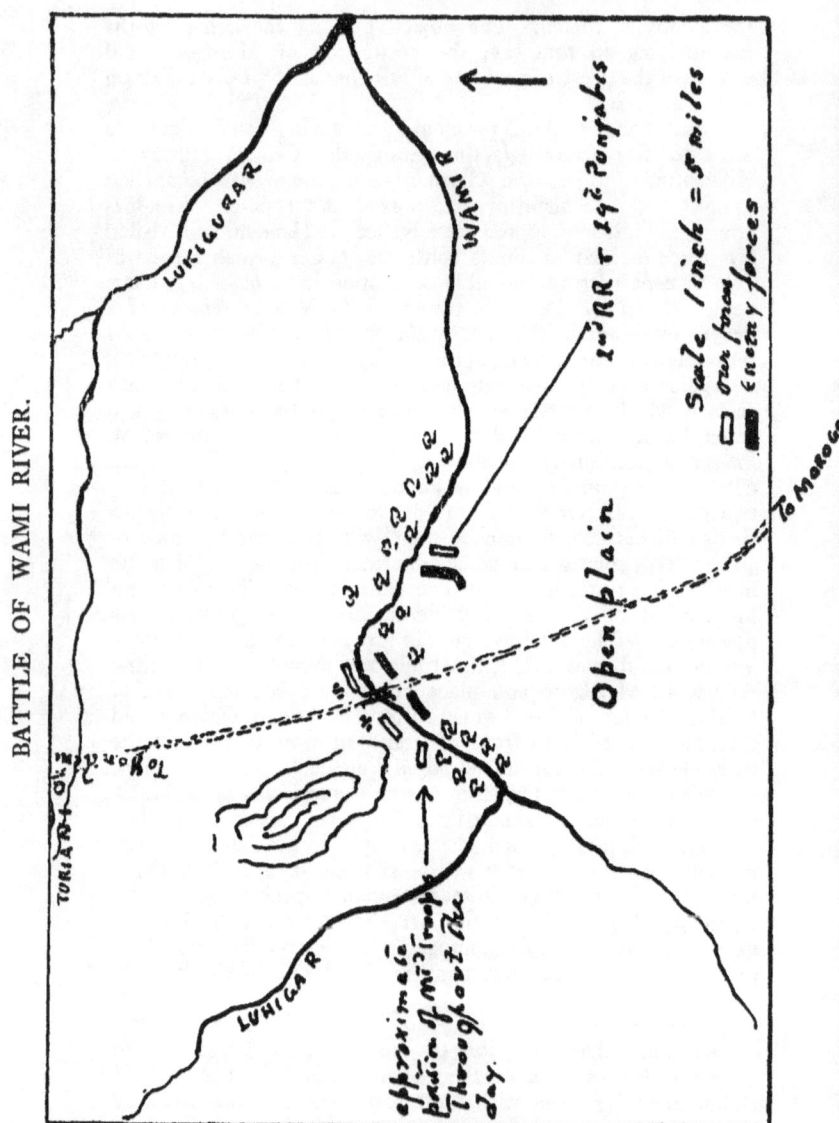

BATTLE OF WAMI RIVER.

gura, making a wide movement round the enemy's left flank by way of the Borama river, reaching Turiani on the 8th; Hannington's brigade to march via Mahasi to Turiani, reaching there on the 9th; General Sheppard's brigade (1st East African) to clear the enemy out of Ruhungu and Kanga—a big task, as the brigade then mustered but 1,400 rifles. The Rhodesia Regiment were 300 strong in camp, but worn and emaciated. Surg.-Major Hurst medically inspected the Regiment on the 6th, pronouncing 86 men unfit to march, and many others doubtful. In this contingency it seemed best to form one Company of 120 picked fit men, with four machine-guns, and to eliminate headquarters, orderly-room, armourer, cook, tailor, and indeed the whole Staff; in fact, it was necessary, as nearly all our first-line transport mules had succumbed to fly-sickness, leaving us immobile as a regiment. It was a compact and efficient little Company of Rhodesians, that marched away under command of Major Coker with the 1st East African Brigade in the early morning of August 7th: further, we practically replaced the Divisional Staff that had all gone down with sickness excepting the Brigade-Major, 1st E.A. Brigade; thus Capt. Blagrove became Staff-Captain, Lieut. Cowper G.S.O.3, and Lieut. Baker Orderly-Officer.

At daybreak on the 7th the Brigade left Msiha before it could be observed by the watchers on the frowning hills and started down the right bank of the Lukigura river. It would, of course, have been futile to have approached the Ruhungu position by the main road, obstructed as it was by every description of obstacle, fallen trees, mines, abattis, carpet boma, *chevaux de frise* sited with uncommon skill.

The Brigade returned on the 8th without encountering the enemy—its task unaccomplished; for the difficult, almost impossible country met with precluded the contemplated attack on the enemy's left flank.

On the early morning of the 9th, the 1st East African Brigade, constituted as before, again marched out, but with a different task set: it was to march down the banks of the Lukigura to the Wami river on the flank of the enemy now retiring from Ruhungu on Morogoro, via Turiani and Wami, The good work of Hannington's brigade on the enemy's right flank—the fight it valiantly fought—and the march of Britz's mounted brigade to Turiani, hardly enter into the scope of this chronicle. Simply let it be said that the enemy with his guns slipped through Turiani almost unmolested.

On Wednesday, August 16th, transport oxen arrived at Msiha—only 16 survived of the 76 that left Taveta with the regiment—enabling Headquarters and Staff to start at 3 a.m. on the 17th to catch up the brigade that had marched to Wami without encountering opposition but on crossing to and turning up the right bank of the river had come in contact with the right flank guard of the enemy, who was making a stand by holding the right bank, having destroyed the large bridge over the river on the main road to Morogoro. In this fight the Company of Rhodesians was held in reserve, until an Indian regiment forming the firing line, and fighting splendidly, had been so battered and shaken that it required stiffening. There was no one like the Rhodesians for the job : in perfectly extended order they advanced, and threw themselves into the gaps between files of their Indian comrades, where shoulder to shoulder, cheek by jowl they carried on. It was the fight of the individual, a soldier's battle, for once the men had been committed to their task, they necessarily disappeared from the eye, control and leadership of their officers ; and yet one and all did well, did all and more than was required of them. Towards evening the enemy broke off an indecisive engagement. Our casualties, considering the small number of men engaged, were heavy : Killed, Lieut. S. Cartwright (8th Northampton Regiment) attached, No. 816 Corpl. V. M. Cox, 662 Pte. V. C. Alexander, 421 Pte. G. M. White, 1281 Pte. R. A. Seward ; wounded, Lieut. (Temp.-Capt.) W. O. McCarthy, 1118 Pte. H. S. Winter, 1234 Pte. E. E. Reinecke, 1608 Pte. J. R. Davis, 974 Pte. W. S. G. Coxwell, 1529 Pte. J. McCall, 1504 J. Colley, 771 L.-Corpl. P. Gallagher, 1458 Pte. W. Jasper. Also one machine-gun porter killed and three wounded.

The loss of McCarthy, ex-farmer of Shamva, who died of his wounds, was deeply mourned by the Regiment ; he had long commanded a Company, and was beloved by all ranks. Cartwright, an experienced soldier, was in civil life assistant-magistrate at Bulawayo, a trained and skilful machine-gun officer, and could ill be spared. Of the others it need only be said that they were of our best, the best that Rhodesia offered—too often the sacrifice was accepted.

It has been shown how, and why, firstly the operations round Moshi and Taveta ; secondly, how those round Ruhungu and the Nguru hills failed to inflict a crushing defeat on the enemy forces, although Smuts had reasonable and well-founded grounds for expecting them to be decisive, for his plans were admirable to that end. Thirdly, as soon as he learnt of the enemy stand on the Wami, he formulated a simple but comprehensive scheme, that properly executed should have brought utter defeat to the enemy, stated to be seven companies, probably totalling 1,600 rifles, holding the south bank of the river, and roughly forty miles distant from their base at Morogoro. The 1st East African Brigade was ordered to attack the right flank, and did so with courage and determination. Another force advanced to the river bank, and held the enemy for hours on the hither brink.

We had a Mounted Brigade: Where was it? What is it doing?—those were the questions on every lip, and in our thoughts and minds; on the lips and in the thoughts of the enemy also. What *are* they doing? So much were these questions in the enemy's thoughts that they were obsessed by them, their action influenced by them, that a prisoner captured by the 1st E.A. Brigade stated that seven companies had orders to destroy their arms at 3 p.m. and then surrender.

The enemy knew we had a Mounted Brigade, and no doubt expected it to be in its proper place, the place ordained by the rules of war, and to have done the proper thing, the thing done by British troops for ages gone. They pictured it as having crossed the Wami well clear of either of their flanks, as having placed themselves in rear of them, on the wide open plain between the Wami and Ngerengere river (some thirty miles south), country adapted in every way to the successful use of mounted troops.

But nothing happened. Our infantry and our guns fought on bravely, asking themselves: " How long will it be before the mounted troops take their place and share in the battle? "—and enemy guns and rifles jeered: " How long? " The enemy retiring their guns found their rear unthreatened, countermanded the order for surrender of their gallant companies, and substituted one " for an orderly retirement on Morogoro "; and an orderly and unmolested retirement they made—there was nothing elusive about it. The infantry could not pursue, they were fagged out; they had marched far to the fight that had lasted for long hours, during which they had lain in the burning sun-scorched veldt, killing and being killed, wounding and being wounded. Further, the bulk of the infantry was on the wrong side of the river, and would have had to march some miles to a flank to effect a crossing.

So at evensong the men of the infantry remarked in their weariness nonchalantly: " I wonder what the cavalry were doing? " " Will anyone be shot over this job? " Those two questions simply reflected the opinion formed of the action by the mere onlooker and private infantry soldier, possibly misguided and misinformed, but impressionable, and impressed, as they flung themselves down as those that had earned their rest, and knew they had done their best.

CHAPTER XII.

IT was a great stretch of waterless, flat and arid country between the Wami and Ngerengere rivers that the 1st East African Brigade started to cross at 4 p.m. on August 22nd, an expanse on which mounted troops might play havoc with infantry. The latter-named river was reached by the weary and dusty troops at 8.30 p.m. on the 23rd, after a trying and arduous march of some thirty miles, during which the enemy was not met with. That night, terrific explosions were heard in the direction of the railway, some ten miles distant; the enemy were frantically destroying everything of military value in Morogoro. Guns were being scrapped, small arms broken and burnt, ammunition stacked and exploded; on the railway, the permanent way was being torn up, bridges were being destroyed, and rolling-stock rushed over into the rivers below, locomotives being piled up one on another in one great tangled mass of scrap-iron.

The 24th was occupied in reconnoitring; for the country and present dispositions of the enemy were quite unknown to us.

Morogoro, of which I was appointed Military Commandant, was said to be evacuated, so on the early morning of the 25th I was instructed to occupy it with the 2nd Rhodesia Regiment and a half-battalion of 130th K.G.O. Baluchis. The order was looked upon as a compliment to the Regiment, a tribute to its behaviour and discipline; and the fact that we shared the honour with our great friends the Baluchis was a further cause of satisfaction.

The Commander-in-Chief's trust was not misplaced; the gallant Baluchis I posted for the immediate protection of the town, while the Rhodesians were entrusted with the policing and administration of it in all its branches, and herein they displayed a great versatility and handiness; they became provosts, bakers, printers, sheriffs, billeting officers, engine-men, railway officials, and indeed put the whole town machinery, left standing and disorganized by the enemy, into going order.

We found the place looted and being looted by natives, and in dreadful disorder. It had reverted to absolute lawlessness

IN EAST AFRICA

and savage licence in the few hours interregnum between the evacuation by the enemy and our occupation, and natives trundled hand-carts down the streets, piled with erstwhile contents of ladies' wardrobes, carried chairs and tables on their heads, and soft goods in sacks.

A stern measure was necessary summarily to ensure the discontinuance of this state of things; the measure was taken, and looting, sabotage and lawlessness at once came to an end. There were many terrified German women in the town, and not a few able-bodied men, non-combatants; and the hospitals and gaols were full of sick and wounded. To all in those first few days of our occupation the men of the Regiment proved themselves kind, sympathetic, but very firm masters, irreproachable in their conduct, fair and just.

Morogoro was full of deeply-dug shelters, bomb and shell proof; open spaces revealed dark cavernous mouths to stairs leading into chambers in the bowels of the earth, dug-outs of a family capacity, into which the inhabitants were wont to scramble and crawl on the first sound of our aeroplanes that consistently bombed Turiani and Morogoro during our enforced sojourn in Msiha or " Shell Camp."

On August 26th, the G.O.C. with his Staff and Generals Britz and Van de Venter arrived in Morogoro.

On the 27th a reconnoitring patrol of forty 2nd Rhodesia Regiment under Capt. Hare scouted through the hills immediately south of the town, but only located a small enemy picket watching proceedings below.

Capt. Smith, the Adjutant, applied to resign in order to rejoin his regiment, the 12th Lancers, and I reluctantly recommended his application; he had done good and loyal work for the Regiment from the day he joined it in Salisbury in 1914.

On August 27th, the Baluchis were ordered to rejoin the Brigade still in pursuit of the enemy—an enemy now scattered and dispersed by recent operations, becoming more elusive, nomadic, and more difficult to locate; splitting into smaller and independent columns, as a prelude to inevitable guerilla tactics, maintained until the Great Armistice was signed; tactics involving many British columns, chasing a will-o'-the-wisp with a deadly sting in its tail.

On August 30th the 2nd Rhodesia Regiment were ordered to rejoin the Brigade, already on the road to Kissaki; and what remained of it, left under command of Major Jesser-Coope, who had recently returned to the Regiment. Myself as Military Commandant, with Lieut. Griffith as Staff Officer, and many details fulfilling jobs and posts that were essential, had to remain at Morogoro, until L.-of-C. troops arrived to relieve us. The Regiment caught up the Brigade at the Massimbisi river on September 1st and marched with it to the Ruwu river, where the enemy had destroyed the bridge spanning 150 feet of swift water running between high and steep banks. From there on, and for many days, the Regiment was occupied in the building and constructing of bridges and roads—always on short rations and hard work, living to a large extent on the native foods of the country, toiling long hours and sleeping short.

In front, the 2nd East African Brigade kept in touch with an enemy persistently and slowly retiring towards Kissaki. Rain fell steadily, and seldom the sun shone to dry the sodden kits. It was not until October 1st that the 2nd Rhodesia Regiment ceased their road-making and invaluable construction work and marched from Summit camp to rejoin the remainder of the Brigade at Tulo, thirteen miles onward; but on arrival there it was learnt that the Brigade had moved on to Duthumi, twelve miles forward. On arrival at Duthumi the Regiment was met by the Staff-Captain, who informed us that the Headquarters of the Brigade was at Dakawa, and the enemy were holding the southern bank of the Mgeta river, and that the 2nd Rhodesia Regiment would form a post at Kwa-Hongo, a thousand yards or so from the enemy lines on the southern bank. And this they did, digging in and entrenching a camp, making shift with a little dirty water out of pools, no sugar, and only half-rations of tea and flour. The Lines of Communication had become more attentuated as they became longer, and the enemy denied us the water of the Mgeta River.

The 29th Punjabis, under Colonel Ford, and 3rd Kashmir Rifles had established themselves on the southern bank of the Mgeta, but in the face of a strong concentration opposite them, their withdrawal was decided upon. Four officers, 40 rifles, and 2 machine-guns was all the 2nd Rhodesia Regiment could muster to help them out of their difficult position, leaving only 13 rifles and 2 machine-guns to defend Kwa-Hongo post; but the withdrawal was satisfactorily effected in the still and stuffy night, with little or no loss. The 3rd Kashmir Rifles were also ordered to retire across the river, and in this connection an interesting little incident occurred, for the Commanding Officer, Major Money, on effecting the retirement and finding the few available Rhodesians in position and covering them, exclaimed, in the darkness: " Oh! it's you! The good old Rhodesians always come to help us when we are in a hole!!!"

For some days now, opposing forces on either side of the Mgeta shelled and shot at each other ; patrol "incidents" were of daily occurrence, but without any definite results.

On Sunday, October 15th, I rejoined the Regiment at Kwa-Hongo, as I had been enabled to hand over the command of Morogoro on the arrival there of L.-of-C. troops. I found only 125 rifles of the 2nd Rhodesia Regiment still going strong, and of these Major Jesser-Coope had evidently made the most.

On the 16th the 2nd Rhodesia Regiment marched to Duthumi, and I took over that post from Lieut.-Col. Ross of the West Africa Frontier Force, who were holding it.

The state of the Regiment about this time is succinctly reflected in the following letter, a copy of which was sent to me :—

CONFIDENTIAL.

DAKAWA, Oct. 26th, 1916.

The Senior Medical Officer yesterday carefully inspected the 2nd Rhodesia Regiment.

53 men were doing duty. Of these, only 30 were really *fit* for duty.

120 men are reported to be arriving shortly, as reinforcements. Most of these are men discharged from hospital, who will not stay long out of hospital at Duthumi.

Even after the arrival of this Draft, it is doubtful whether the Regiment will muster 100 men fit to take the field. The question of the retention of such a fragment of a unit is (as in the case of the 29th Punjabis) rather Imperial than personal.

The men of the 2nd Rhodesia Regiment enlisted "for the period of the war." If allowed to recoup itself in time, the Regiment will probably be fit to render very useful service, in some other theatre of war, in a few months' time.

But if it is kept in the field until it simply ceases to exist it is unlikely ever to recover.

The Regiment has done such good work, often under very trying circumstances, during its twenty months in East Africa, that it would be sad to see it disappear from sheer exhaustion."

(*Signed*) S. H. SHEPPARD, Brig.-Gen.,
1st E.A. Brigade.

The country between Morogoro and Kisaki, through which we passed and trailed behind us our ever-lengthening and narrowing Lines of Communication, calls for some description. From Morogoro to the Mwuha river, where—three miles to the north Summit camp and field hospital was established—the road was just a rough African veldt track ; from Summit to the Mwuha, a mountain goat path was converted into a deep winding cutting circling in a red earth line down to the river far below; it was here that the Rhodesians had put in so much hard work. From the Mwuha river onwards the low-lying country was clothed in forest and tall elephant-grass, that sprung from swamps and quagmires, across which it was necessary to corduroy the road for miles. Thousands of dead transport animals shared the sides of the road with thousands of dead horses of the S.A.M.R., whose saddles were being carried back to the rear by hundreds of porters. The whole road stank insufferably; every few yards lay a putrefying carcase, every few yards a moving, wriggling, seething mass of maggots. Men spat and smoked and held their breath and noses, but nothing could deny that abominable stench—miles and miles of it. Tsetse flies that had caused this shambles, this indescribable road of nastiness, bit man and beast incessantly as they marched in the steamy heat. No domestic animal or bird lived in this afflicted land; the natives kept no fowls nor goats nor cattle, the fly ruled supreme.

More revolting and disgusting than the stench or the tsetse fly was the great blue blood-red-headed blow-fly in its millions, hatched from the putrid masses that choked the road. As a worn-out man lay and slept in sun or shade these dreadful things would buzz and buzz round him, settle on his hair, his moustache, his clothing, and there lay their dirty cream-white eggs—fly-blow—which in an hour of the fierce heat would be turned into little wriggling maggots. Fly would follow fly and deposit its ova in the same spot, until the waking man, passing his fingers through his hair, would find inch-high clumps of fly-blow and maggots in it, adhering closely, and see the mass on his clothing and in his blankets, and the millions of red-headed horrors still humming round him. Even in murky night a sleeper's unconscious movement would awake that dreadful buzzing and cause the waking man to shudder and squirm in disgust and nausea. But it was war—red, savage and infinitely brutal, sparing neither man nor beast.

The military situation at the time was an interesting one. The 1st East African Brigade, weakened by sickness, fighting, and casualties, mustered only some 1,300 rifles, and comprised the 2nd Rhodesia Regiment, 2nd Kashmir Rifles, 3rd Kashmir Rifles, 130th K.G.O. Baluchis, 29th Punjabis, and the 25th Royal Fusiliers. The Brigade held a line from Tulo to Kissaki, on which there were four main camps, namely :—Duthumi, with the 2nd Rhodesia Regiment, 2nd Kashmir Rifles, and 5th S.A.F.A., and one howitzer; Kwa-Hongo, with 130th Baluchis as garrison; Dakawa, Brigade Headquarters, with 29th Punjabis and two companies of 130th Baluchis; Kissaki with the 25th Royal Fusiliers. Thrown forward to within some eight hundred yards of the Mgeta river is an outpost line strongly entrenched ; on the other and left bank of the river the enemy is similarly entrenched, three to eight hundred yards dividing combatants. The country, covered with thick elephant-grass, precluded the gathering of reliable information ; patrol scraps and intermittent shelling were of daily occurrence. Some eighteen companies primarily opposed us under command of Von Lettow in person ; but later, enemy deserters told us that eight companies were withdrawn to cross the Rufigi river in order to oppose the advance of our troops landed at Kilwa and pressing on the German rear, via Mohoro to Kibambwe, where it was said the enemy had constructed a bridge communicating with their southern base at Utete.

Some anxiety was felt at the time on account of General Northey's column, supposed to be near Mahenge with Van de Venter endeavouring to join it, having marched from Kilossa some weeks before for that purpose. But in the meantime Kraut had taken some companies to oppose Northey, and the German troops from Tabora were at the same time marching against him ; he was known to be in an isolated position with very long Lines of Communication. How this distinguished soldier and the troops under him coped with the situation, is quite another story.

Britz's Mounted Brigade had practically been put out of action by tsetse fly, and the time was near when only native troops would be used, with their sprinkling of European leaders—fighting against an enemy army split into guerila bands, marching hard and fighting hard, in a country infested with fly and fever.

The enemy army proper had been forced to renounce its entity, and was quickly losing cohesion, with bits of it marching hither and thither in bewilderment, but each portion willing to fight when driven into a corner, and anxious to attack if an off-chance of success or plunder offered. In the end destined to unite in one small body under their capable and brave leader Von Lettow, a guerilla band, a will-o'-the-wisp with that deadly sting in its tail. It was during the fighting on the Rufigi river and about Kilwa that General Smuts, called to a higher sphere in the concerns of the Empire, handed over the command in East Africa to General Hoskins—handed over a situation still bristling with the difficulties attending perhaps the most trying campaign ever fought in a tropical country ; left him to battle with an enemy punished, scattered, but unbeaten.

But to leave the great affairs to be described by an historian, and to hark back to those affecting the Rhodesians. The 2nd

Kashmir Rifles, under Lieut.-Col. Lyall, old friends of Mzima days of long ago, again came under my command at Duthumi; they were forming the advanced entrenched line of outposts, in touch with the enemy on the Mgeta.

During the days that followed, patrol encountered patrol; our planes bombed the enemy positions and indicated targets for the fire of our howitzers and the guns of the 5th S.A.F.A. stationed at Duthumi; the enemy shelled consistently our outpost line of 2nd Kashmiris, and occasionally our huts and hospitals at Duthumi; but it is doubtful if much damage was done to either side.

One of the enemy road-mines blew to pieces No. 17 Native Scout, Corpl. Chinanti, on Friday, October 20th; he was escorting a party of surrounded or deserted Askari from Duthumi to Tulo. This native was a Christian, and was accorded a military funeral. On the same date Major Jesser-Coope, who had been ill for some days, was sent to hospital on the L.-of-C. The strength has dwindled down to 102 effectives.

We had occupied Duthumi on October 16th, and from then to December 14th spent more or less uneventful days. Fortunately there was plenty of work on the road—escorts to convoys, picquets, and almost daily patrol affairs, and bombardments; on this date General Sheppard informed me he had received a wire from the G.O.C.-in-Chief saying there was trouble at Lindi, and that as I had only a diminished command, he wished me to take command of the 2nd Battalion West India Regiment, Lindi area, and coastal ports of Kiswere, Sudi Bay, and Mikindani. So on December 16th, 1916, I regretfully said good-bye to the staunch little remnant of Rhodesians at Duthumi, and with confidence handed the command over to Major Coker.

My own affairs and doings at and about Lindi hardly enter the purview of this chronicle, and it need only be said that I became in time to be proud of the battalion that it was my privilege to command—they were smart and they were brave—and that when I left them on March 11th to rejoin the 2nd Rhodesia Regiment on their returning to Rhodesia, I received the following wireless message, far away on the midnight sea: " All ranks of 2nd Battalion West India Regiment wish you good-luck and God-speed."

A day or two before I left Duthumi a little incident occurred that should be put on record, although it affords an anecdote at my expense. Corpl. Stidolph, old soldier, strict disciplinarian, sparse of speech, was on outpost duty, commanding by night a picquet on the road; a big male lion prowled around closely and persistently and became so menacing that Stidolph determined to move his picquet some distance. On hearing of this in the morning, I asked him : " But why didn't you shoot the brute ? " His respectful answer: " I was on outpost duty, sir !—not big-game hunting."

The last military operation in which the Rhodesians were destined to share was imminent when, on December 21st, the Medical Officers examined an attenuated group of men styled the 2nd Rhodesia Regiment. Of that small group he pronounced 37 men as unfit to proceed any further; and to accentuate the discomfiture of his verdict, Lieut. H. O. Frielinghaus arrived from Morogoro reporting that the 61 details there had been examined, and of those, one only, Corpl. Hart, was pronounced as fit for active service. Hart, of sixty-two years, the oldest man in the regiment—who had never failed, never fallen out of the ranks, never reported sick—an example on every march, a trusted comrade in every fight. He had been to Morogoro to have his teeth seen to, and now returned to run in the last lap.

On December 31st three converging columns marched towards the Rufigi, one starting from Tulo, one from Kissaki, and one from Dakawa. The 2nd Rhodesia Regiment—now 91 rifles and 4 machine-guns—were held in general reserve at Duthumi.

On January 1st, 1917, the bombardment of the German trenches opposite Duthumi commenced. The long 4-inch guns that we had so anxiously waited for in vain at Msiha had at last arrived, after their four months rest in Morogoro ; they now opened the ball.

The enemy left their position on the Mgeta, and the 1st Nigerian battalion occupied it at 5 p.m.

In the meanwhile Col. Lyall's column had got astride the Kiderengwa-Behobeho road near Tshimbe, and engaging the retiring enemy, captured a 4·1-inch howitzer and many prisoners.

At 2.30 p.m., January 2nd, the 2nd Rhodesia Regiment left Duthumi for Tshimbe, which they took over from Col. Lyall at 5.30 a.m. on January 3rd, together with 3 European and 95 Askari prisoners, one howitzer and a quantity of stores.

It was during this fighting about Behobeho that Capt. F. C. Selous, 25th Royal Fusiliers, was killed, gallant and game to the last ; a great Rhodesian.

On January 5th the Rhodesians were ordered to rejoin their Brigade at Kimbambwe on the Rufigi, but were delayed at Tchogowali until the 9th, in a very unhealthy camp that had evidently been long occupied by a large force of the enemy.

General Sheppard had crossed the Rufigi at Kimbambwe

with little opposition, but when the 30th Punjabis had made good the crossing they were heavily attacked and suffered severely ; on receiving reinforcements they were able to hold their ground.

The operations—the last to be planned by General Smuts, the last to be participated in by the 2nd Rhodesia Regiment— were well conceived and brilliantly carried out, but there was no hope or prospect of their being decisive, by reason of the dense nature of the country, and the many existing avenues for retirement ; it was possible to harass, disperse and punish severely, and this was efficiently and effectively done.

It was now decided that the Rufigi valley was no place in which to retain European troops already war-worn, lantern-jawed, emaciated, and drenched with fever ; so two small bodies of gaunt men turned from the Rufigi towards Morogoro at 5 a.m. on January 11th, 1917 ; they were styled respectively the 25th Royal Fusiliers and the 2nd Rhodesia Regiment.

CHAPTER XIII.

SO the last long march of the Rhodesians commenced on January 11th, 1917, when reluctantly they turned their ragged backs on the Rufigi and the enemy. They little realized that they had turned homewards only to be disbanded on arrival ; to be deprived of their hard-won entity ; to be lost in countless units eddying in the vortex of war. That the Regiment should cease to exist before the cessation of hostilities never entered the head of any man serving in East Africa.

Thus in ignorance and hope they retraced their steps in glorious expectation of a holiday well earned, brief but jolly, in their beloved Homeland. They marched through insanitary Tchogowali ; through Dakawa, erstwhile Brigade Headquarters ; Duthumi, fraught with memories of a long tarrying and much sickness, and now but one vast hospital on the Lines of Communication.

At-long-last, on January 21st, they reached the railway at Mikesse and entrained for Morogoro, 91 of all ranks out of a strength of 800. Followed a protracted stay in Morogoro. Rumour trod on the heels of rumour ; the Regiment was destined for service in Egypt ; it was returning to Rhodesia ; it was still urgently required in East Africa—each in turn gained ascendency and credence.

On March 13th I returned to Dar-es-Salaam from Lindi and resumed command of the Regiment, taking over from Major Coker, in whom I had rightly placed my confidence when I handed it over to him at Duthumi on December 15th.

An effort was now made by certain authorities to capture our regimental native scouts, and also our machine-gun porters. The former, recruited in Rhodesia, had done splendid work throughout—always cheerful, always willing, accepting the risks that all scouts must, with a native's *sang-froid*. Thus they had endeared themselves and won the respect of a Regiment that throughout had known no colour bar, and that treated as comrades those that were brave. I refused staunchly to leave them in a land of strangers.

The porters had served us faithfully in many a tight corner, had risked their lives over and over for a stake in which they had no part ; for these I was able to procure two months' leave and a promise that they would be transferred *en bloc* to a King's African Rifles battalion.

Finally, on March 29th, definite orders were received that the Regiment would return to Rhodesia to recuperate, and what there was of it at Morogoro left there on the 30th and arrived at Dar-es-Salaam at 6 p.m. the same day, and was put under canvas in the Imperial Detail Camp—and very inferior canvas at that, pitched in a swampy palm grove. There were no arrangements made for the reception of troops from the firing-line or the front. All houses were the perquisites of the innumerable Staff and Departments, whose members all lived in luxury under electric lights in villas or mansions and with plenty of food. Fighting-men, when they arrived, appeared to be considered a nuisance, to be pitched into a pestilential palm grove until happily disburdened.

We did not clear out as soon as the Staff expected or wished, because the alleged presence of an enemy raider along the coast dislocated shipping, and it was not until April 8th that the Regiment embarked on H.M.S. *Himalaya*.

Capt. Tribe and many non-commissioned officers and men remained behind, some joining the King's African Rifles, others the Intelligence or some other Department.

Everything possible was done by Capt. Colin McKenzie and the officers and crew of the *Himalaya* to promote the comfort and well-being of the Regiment.

The *Himalaya* was acting as escort to the S.S. *Nile*, *Kinfauns Castle*, and *Aragon* ; the last an ill-fated ship carrying a Cape Labour Corps, of whom 16 were buried at sea on April 9th, 6 on the 10th, and the same number on the 11th. We had ourselves 84 men on the sick list, mostly malarial cases.

Our days on H.M.S. *Himalaya* were made so enjoyable that we were almost sorry to disembark on Friday, April 13th, at Beira, where the British residents hospitably received us.

Rhodesia laid itself out to give us a hearty welcome back ; loyal Umtali, our border town, extending a very warm reception.

The magnificent greeting which the Regiment received at Salisbury on its arrival at 6 p.m. on April 14th cannot be better described than by the insertion of the following articles published in the *Rhodesia Herald* :—

Rhodesia Herald, Monday, April 16, 1917.

OUR REGIMENT.

Rhodesia is represented in most of the war theatres in which British troops are employed. Rhodesians have done particularly good work with the Northern Column, commanded by the gallant Colonel

Murray, first on the border, and afterwards under General Northey's command in German East Africa, and also in the Rhodesian platoons of the King's Royal Rifle Corps ; but it is no disparagement of the work these have done and are doing, to say that the people of the territory are especially interested in, and proud of the record of, the 2nd Rhodesia Regiment. It is a distinctively Rhodesian unit, and it has just completed two years of the most arduous campaigning that has fallen to the lot of any regiment. In a message to the officers and men two years ago, on the eve of their departure for East Africa, His Excellency the High Commissioner stated : " I am confident that their services to their King and country will be no less valuable than those which their comrades of the 1st Rhodesia Regiment are rendering with the Union forces, and that, equally with them, they will be an honour to Rhodesia." The confidence of His Excellency and of the people of Rhodesia in the 2nd Rhodesia Regiment has certainly not been misplaced. And our people can endorse whole-heartedly the following passage in the address of welcome presented to Colonel Capell on behalf of the Municipalities and general public on the arrival of the Regiment in Salisbury on Saturday :—

> We congratulate you on the magnificent spirit of duty, valour and endurance exhibited by all ranks in the course of a struggle of unexampled severity, which has earned for your regiment the unstinted praise of all those who have come in contact with it in the field.

And they will also read with cordial approval the spirited address delivered by the Right Rev. the Bishop of Southern Rhodesia at the united thanksgiving service held at the camp yesterday morning, and which we report to-day. General Smuts, in a speech at Pretoria, on his return from East Africa, said : " The South African troops under my command were perfect gentlemen, and I am proud of them." This testimony applies no less to the 2nd Rhodesians than to the Union Forces. Not only were our men far longer in the field than any other South African corps, but they earned a reputation second to that of no other regiment for gallantry, discipline and chivalrous conduct. They appear to have been notably happy in their relations with the regiments with which they were associated in the field from time to time, whether Imperial, Colonial or Indian, and no less with the brigade commanders under whom they served. But the full value of their services can only be appreciated when the story of the campaign comes to be written. The 2nd Rhodesia Regiment arrived in East Africa at a rather critical juncture, and we believe the historian will do adequate justice to the great services it rendered in assisting to thwart the German plans to overrun British East Africa. The officers and men of the Regiment have earned and no doubt require a period of recuperative leave. We hope their stay in Rhodesia may prove pleasant and invigorating and will fit them for the strenuous work that lies before them in Europe or Egypt. Their fellow colonists will watch the future of the Regiment with profound interest and with the utmost confidence that it will add fresh laurels to those won in East Africa. We are very much gratified to find that the welcome that has been extended to the Regiment has assumed something of a national character ; and we feel sure that it must be a source of pleasure to the officers and men as it is to the people of Salisbury that the Mayors of Rhodesia and the Chairmen of the minor municipal bodies should be officially identified with the movement. This circumstance serves to show how keen is the pride and how great is the attachment of the people of the country to those who have so worthily represented them on the battlefields of East Africa and will shortly be called on to play an equally distinguished and hazardous role in one of the other war theatres.

Rhodesia Herald, Monday, April 16, 1917.

THE RETURN OF THE RHODESIANS.

If enthusiasm ran high on the occasion of the departure of the 2nd Rhodesia Regiment for East Africa, it reached fever heat on Saturday night when the gallant men returned. Following upon a week of hopes and disappointments, when rumour ran riot and the wildest of stories filled the air, Saturday's scene at the railway station was a fitting climax to an exciting week. The reception was worthy of the splendid men in whose honour it was promoted, and a magnificent indication of the real spirit of the people and their generous hospitality. The main street leading to the station was gaily decorated with festoons and bunting, while upon a glaring background of blazing red calico the one word which filled all hearts was lifted high above the entrance gates— Welcome. It was a salutation more genuinely sincere because of its simplicity. It rang true and honest, and conveyed to the returning warriors the kindliest thoughts of the people whose hearts ached with a throbbing emotion, and whose very being thrilled with joy at the fact that our boys had come home once more. There were no blatant symbols of false sentimentality or mock heroics. They were unnecessary, and in any case their presence would have marred the picture which in all other respects was a complete reflection of the depth of the people's welcome. The sun had gone down just before the crowd swayed with excitement and intense pent-up emotion thrilled at the glad news, " The train is rounding the curve." It was just the moment when the beautiful but flitting twilight of Rhodesia lent the one touch of sentiment, properly so-called, which harmonised with the scene and softly illuminated the upturned joyous faces of the dense crowd who had waited so long for that precise minute. The long train drew slowly along the platform the windows of each carriage packed with khaki clad figures, only by now dimly discernible in the rapidly failing light.

THE BRITISH CHEER.

There was no cheering for several long moments, and then the realisation of the situation broke on all, returned veterans and crowd alike. The murmur of a cheer rose in soft cadence from the far end of the line, and as it rose it took courage, swelled in volume, and from thousands of throats the real, solid British cheer burst forth in all its fullness. It was a glorious moment. The heart of Salisbury was flung into that cheer, and then it broke down. That was the pathetic moment. Tears diffused the eyes of men and women alike, but none would have had it otherwise. Men caught their throats to choke the sob which in any case was bound to force its way upwards, and then they cheered again. They must have completely broken down had not a kindly nature so gently relieved those tense feelings. It was good to see it all and to experience something of that thrill which shook the crowd. God bless our lads!

That was the one predominant note which was struck, and how much it meant only perhaps the boys themselves knew in their souls. Such moments occur rarely in one's life and one is the better for them. The British people are notoriously phlegmatic, but on those all too infrequent occasions when they are released from their bondage in this respect, their high feelings and buoyant enthusiasm know no bounds. Such an occasion occurred on Saturday night, and it was a red-letter day in the history of the Capital.

THE ENCLOSURE.

There was a little enclosure erected on the spacious platform in which the more prominent townspeople of Salisbury were privileged guests of the Mayor. It was gaily bedecked with bunting and greenery, and an additional splash of colour was lent to the gathering by the presence of men in uniform and the Mayors of Salisbury, Bulawayo, and Umtali resplendent in their mayoral gowns of carmine hue, and wearing their somewhat cumbrous chains of office. An open space directly in front of the enclosure was kept clear by the members of the Southern Rhodesia Volunteers, Rhodesia Volunteer Reserves and Cadets, with fixed bayonets, and here presently the members of the 2nd Rhodesia Regiment were to assemble to receive the grateful thanks and, let it at once be admitted, the homage of the citizens. Around this square the people of Salisbury surged, men, women and children, and in the background a somewhat sombre looking but loyal crowd of natives held the edge of the throng. They chanted, perhaps a trifle mournfully, their song of welcome, but it was none the less sincere on that account.

GUARD OF HONOUR.

Drawn up on the station platform were the stalwarts of the 1st and 2nd Rhodesia Platoons, some of whom have not yet been blooded, but if their grand physiques are an indication of their potentialities as fighters for the Empire, they cannot fail to enhance the laurels which have been won for the country by the men whom we delight in honouring to-day. The platoons constituted the guard of honour, and they were under the command of the man who has been responsible for the general efficiency of the Regiment which has just returned, Captain Blatherwick. As soon as the train stopped, the band of the Southern Rhodesia Volunteers, under Mr. Bater, sounded the initial note of welcome, and the troops presented arms. A few moments later the 2nd Rhodesia Regiment fell in on their markers on the square. They have returned cheerful and confident, but despite their sunburnt faces and arms there are many to whom the recuperation now to be afforded them will be most gladly welcomed. They bear the marks of their experiences. The rigours of an East African climate for two years have told their tale on the stamina of our men, yet they were proud in their bearing as they stood to attention to receive the thanks of the community for work magnificently performed and gratitude for their return.

PROMINENT PEOPLE PRESENT.

His Honour the Administrator is still too unwell to leave his bed following his recent accident, and his absence was sympathetically regretted by all present. There were, however, present in the enclosure: Lady Chaplin, His Honour the Resident Commissioner, Messrs. F. J. Newton, C. H. Tredgold, E. W. S. Montagu, and Dr. Nobbs, representing the Government; their Worships the Mayors of Salisbury, Bulawayo and Umtali, and representatives from Gatooma, Hartley and other centres, the Right Rev. the Bishop of Southern Rhodesia, the Rev. James Craig (representing the Presbyterian Church), the Rev. Fathar Parry (Catholic Church), the Rev. Fred. Conquer (the Wesleyans), the Rev. M. M. Levy (Jewish community), General Edwards, the Commandant-General, Sir Charles Coghlan, Col. R. Grey, Mr. M. E. Cleveland, Mr. L. Cripps, Mr. E. A. Begbie, Mr. J. McChlery, representing the Legislative Council, Colonel Masterman, heads of departments, representatives of local public bodies, and other prominent townspeople and many ladies.

THE COMMANDANT-GENERAL.

When the Regiment had paraded under Colonel Capell, the Commanding Officer, the Commandant-General addressed the Regiment. He said : Colonel Capell, officers, non-commissioned officers and men of the 2nd Rhodesia Regiment. I have already communicated to you His Excellency the High Commissioner's welcome. I will, however, read it to you again. It is as follows : " Will be glad if you will convey to the officers and men of the 2nd Rhodesia Regiment my welcome on their return and my congratulations on the splendid work they have done in East Africa. I hope that they will enjoy the rest they have so thoroughly earned, and that after reorganisation they will win fresh honours for themselves and Rhodesia in other fields." I wish His Honour the Administrator was here to give you words of welcome. He is, unfortunately, laid up as the result of an accident, and he cannot come. He has, however, asked me to express to you his warmest welcome, and to congratulate you most heartily on the fine record you have made whilst on active service ; to wish you a happy time while you are here recuperating, and to express the hope that you may get well soon and return to the front, where every man is required at this most serious crisis of the war. He asked me to read to you the following message from the Directors of the British South Africa Company : " Please convey to Colonel Capell and the 2nd Rhodesians the Board's warmest congratulations on their return to Rhodesia for a well-earned rest after two years' arduous service." Before I conclude I would like to add my own congratulations and good wishes and those of the Southern Rhodesia troops in this country. We have watched you officers and men with interest, and at times with anxiety. We are thoroughly proud of you, and we trust and hope that you will soon get fit and well again.

His Worship the Mayor of Salisbury then received the officers of the Regiment and said : On behalf of the citizens I wish to welcome you back to Rhodesia and to present to you an address of welcome from the representative bodies in Rhodesia. The Town Clerk will read the address.

ADDRESS OF WELCOME.

The Town Clerk then read the following address which was signed by the Mayors and Town Clerks of Salisbury, Bulawayo, Gwelo and Umtali, the Chairman of the Village Management Board, Hartley, and the Chairman of the Sanitary Board, Gatooma :—

" Sir,—On behalf of the Municipalities and the people of Rhodesia, we, the undersigned, beg to offer to you and to the gallant officers, non-commissioned officers and men under your command a most hearty welcome on your return from your strenuous campaign in East Africa.

" We congratulate you on the magnificent spirit of duty, valour and endurance exhibited by all ranks in the course of a struggle of unexampled severity, which has earned for your Regiment the unstinted praise of all those who have come in contact with it in the field.

" We can assure you that the people of Rhodesia have watched with deep pride and intense sympathy every movement of your Regiment, and that, while we deplore the loss of so many of your brave comrades, we feel that your great sacrifices and theirs have contributed in an inestimable degree to the victory over His Majesty's unscrupulous enemies and set up for your Regiment an imperishable monument of heroism and devotion.

"We trust that your temporary stay in Rhodesia will enable you so to recuperate after your severe trials that you will shortly be able to uphold in another sphere the great honour which you have won, and which, we feel confident, is safe in your keeping."

COL. CAPELL'S REPLY.

Colonel Capell, in reply, said: Your Honour, my Lord Bishop, your Worships the Mayors of Rhodesia, the Commandant-General, ladies and gentlemen,—It is my duty on behalf of the Regiment which it has been my infinite pride to command for over $2\frac{1}{4}$ years, to thank you, first His Honour the Administrator for having sent such a kind message of welcome to the Regiment. It will be highly appreciated always. Secondly, I thank you, on behalf of the Regiment, for the address which has been presented by the principal civic representatives of the larger towns of Southern Rhodesia. The address, which I have just handed to be in charge of a small guard, will always be a valued treasure of the Regiment to record. It is full of praise. I hope some of it is deserved. I should like to be convinced that the whole lot is deserved; but we have not finished our job yet. We shall have another verdict on it when we have finished our job. In speaking now with so many representatives of the towns of Rhodesia and the people of Rhodesia present, I think I am addressing Rhodesia and its representatives. I would like to tell you how we always felt that we were intimately in touch with Rhodesia when we were in East Africa. In all sorts of places; in all sorts of situations, in lonely places, and in the bush, wherever we have been, we have always felt that Rhodesia is our parent. She has indeed been a regular parent to us, and she has kept in touch with us. I want to thank her for her help and for the encouragement that she has given to us in thought, word and deed. There is one other thing I would like to mention. In the address which we have just received I notice the words "unscrupulous enemy" of His Majesty. Well, as a Britisher, and speaking to Britishers on behalf of Britishers, I wish to say, and it is only fair for me to tell you, that he is not an unscrupulous enemy that we have been fighting in East Africa.

BRITISH GENEROSITY.

It is true that at the beginning of the war in East Africa, for the first month or two, some Askaris got out of hand and there were isolated cases of breaches of the laws of war. Even some of the men of our own Regiment were mutilated; but I think the Regiment has forgiven them. For the last one and a half years the Askaris and the Germans in East Africa have fought with ungloved hands, but with clean hands. They have shown a very sporting spirit. Another thing I noticed, and that is the impression that we have gained a full victory in East Africa. It would be ungenerous to the General who has taken over, General Hoskens, to say that we have got a full victory. The situation handed over to him, in the opinion of everyone who has been there and thought over it, and is capable of forming an opinion, is that the military situation is bristling with tactical and strategical difficulties. It will tax the powers of a very clever General to finish the campaign successfully. There is no doubt about it.

I wish we could have finished the campaign. It is hard luck not being in at the kill, but there is no doubt that after two years in a climate such as East Africa, a white regiment is finished. The stamina is knocked out of it; but as you have kindly suggested, we hope, and we are very keen, to go to another theatre, very keen indeed. I think our secret wish is Flanders. I do not think there is anything else to add, except to thank you, and I do thank Rhodesia for the very kind praise which you have given to us, and that praise is very acceptable indeed to us. But as we have not yet finished our job, we accept it with diffidence. I would only like to say that your Regiment has done its duty. It is your Regiment, and I am not bragging about it. It is not my show, it is your show, and it has done its duty in every sort of situation and circumstances in the campaign, in the field, on the road, building bridges, swimming rivers, crossing rivers; it has never failed me, and I believe it has never failed the officer who has been in command of the troops up there. It has done nothing startling; nothing that we wish to brag about. It has done its plain and simple duty, and absolutely nothing more. If I may say so, I think that Rhodesia, too, has done its duty by the Regiment.

On the call of the Mayor of Salisbury, hearty cheers were raised for the Regiment and renewed, and cheers were afterwards raised by the Regiment for "Our parent, Rhodesia."

Altogether 11 officers and 259 men returned, accompanied by 22 natives, who left with the Regiment and have done invaluable service as scouts. On the same train one officer and two men belonging to the Northern Column, and 25 natives also returned to Salisbury.

The Regiment, headed by the Volunteer Band, left the station in column of fours, taking the salute from the Volunteers and Reserves as they departed. They passed through long lines of cheering townspeople, and eventually arrived at the Police Camp, where an acceptable dinner awaited them. They were afterwards allowed leave, and most of the men returned to town to renew old friendships. Altogether Salisbury assumed a new atmosphere for the remainder of the evening.

* * * *

Little remains to be written. Many officers and men left on well-earned furlough, others were examined by Medical Boards, and invalided from the Service or sent away on recuperative leave.

On July 19th, 1917, we were informed that the Regiment would cease to exist as such, and would be split up to serve as reinforcements to Union troops overseas. No more disastrous or unpopular announcement—from our point of view—could have been made. Bewildered, belittled, pained and disgusted, tradition and *esprit de corps* ravished—officers and men of "our Regiment" applied for transfers to other Units, for other work; tried all sorts of expedients for getting discharges. And the Regiment that would have clung together in all or any circumstances, except disinheritance, began quickly to disintegrate.

IN EAST AFRICA

Can it be wondered at that the Regiment was sore, that it blamed its parent Rhodesia, in its haste and chagrin—blamed her seeming apathy and indifference. Saner and more considered survey shows that only the inevitable happened—that Rhodesia had been drained of her manhood, little by little, drop by drop, until there were no men to fill the depleted ranks of the Regiment; they simply could not be found.

The Commandant-General—Brigadier-General A. H. M. Edwards, C.B., M.V.O., later deservedly knighted for his services—had recruited and trained and sent forward to us in East Africa the last resources of Rhodesia; and when he saw clearly that the Regiment must cease to exist as a formed battalion, he did his utmost, to little avail, to have the identity of the remnants sent overseas, established and maintained. To him, therefore, and to the people of Rhodesia—whom we in the day of disillusionment and disappointment bitterly blamed—we only owe a grateful acknowledgment of services done in their love and pride to and for the Regiment.

On July 9th the remains of the 2nd Rhodesia Regiment entrained for overseas, to be split into a hundred detachments on reaching England; many obtaining commissions, many going down with malaria and sickness born in East Africa, many making the supreme sacrifice before war was ended—all doing their duty.

On October 12th, 1917, an order pronounced officially the disbandment of the 2nd Rhodesia Regiment; and these lines have been written lest it should be forgotten that it ever existed.

APPENDIX I.

PERHAPS to many the following subjoined statistics rendered by the Medical Officer to the Regiment will reflect more vividly than any narrative the nature of the rigorous and withering campaign in which the 2nd Rhodesians played a major part.

It should be stated that the figures given are those of casualties and cases that came under and within the direct treatment of Surgeon-Capt. Ellis, M.C., our own medical officer, with the fighting men, embracing only an average of 300 all ranks in the firing line, and not taking count of the others at bases, in departments, and rest-camps; of those whom in any campaigns will find themselves thitherwards, somewhere away in the rear, on Lines of Communications :—Killed, 36 ; died of wounds or disease, 32 ; wounded, 84; admissions to hospital, 2,272 ; total cases of sickness, comprising malaria 3,127, blackwater 41, dysentery 921, enteric 4, pneumonia 3, amounted to 10,626. Natives, scout and machine-gun porters :—Killed, 6 ; wounded, 8 ; died, 6.

Thirty-six officers and 1,002 rank and file were borne on the books of the Regiment from time to time during its service in East Africa. Thus it will be seen that on an average every member went to hospital twice, and reported sick ten times. But when it is remembered that these statistics only refer to an average of 300 men up in the fighting-front, the vicissitudes of the campaign can be adequately grasped.

APPENDIX II.

ROLL OF THE MEMBERS OF THE 2nd RHODESIA REGIMENT WHO SERVED IN GERMAN EAST AFRICA.

		Attested.	
Lt.-Col.	Capell, D.S.O., Algernon, Essex	1/1/15	Awarded Croix de Guerre, *Lon. Gaz.*, 21/8/17. Mentioned in despatches, *Lon. Gaz.*, 30/6/17.
Major	Cashel, Rowan	24/11/14	
Major	Coker, D.S.O., Harry Oliver	21/11/14	Mentioned in despatches, *Lon. Gaz.*, 8/2/17 and 22/9/17. Awarded D.S.O., *Lon. Gaz.*, 4/6/17.
Major	Jesser-Coope, John Charles	7/1/15	
Captain	Bennett, Walter John	6/11/14	
Captain	Blagrove, John	28/11/14	
Captain	Dodd, Leonard (9th R.W. Kent Regt.) *Attached* 21/3/16		Wounded, 23/8/16.
Captain	Dunn, Alan Johnston	18/11/14	
Captain	Ellis, M.C., Francis Heygate	12/2/15	Awarded M.C., *Lon. Gaz.*, 26/5/17.
Captain	Gordon, George Herschel	25/1/15	
Captain	Hare, M.C., Edgar	26/11/14	
Captain	McCarthy, William Offley	23/12/14	Died of wounds, 26/8/16.
Captain	McQueen, M.C., James	4/2/15	Awarded M.C., *Lon. Gaz.*, 2/2/16. Mentioned in despatches *Lon. Gaz.*, 30/1/17. Died Dodoma, 14/12/17.
Captain	Ogilvie, Hollings Ogilvie	15/1/15	
Captain	Power, D.S.O., Thomas	12/2/15	
Captain	Smith, M.C., Alexander Glegg	1/1/15	Awarded M.C., *Lon. Gaz.*, 30/1/17

THE 2ND RHODESIA REGIMENT

Attested.

Rank	Name	Date	Notes
Captain	Stokes, D.S.O., Francis Maurice William	18/12/14	
Captain	Thomas, M.C., Walter Eric	16/12/14	
Captain	Tribe, Alder Lewis	15/11/14	Wounded, 30/5/16. Killed, 2/9/17.
Lieut.	Allen, Ernest Frank	23/11/14	
Lieut.	Baker, Oswald Trevor	3/11/14	Wounded 12/3/16.
Lieut.	Cartwright, Stanley (8th Northampton Regt.) Attached 18/3/16		Killed, 17/8/16.
Lieut.	Cowper, Charles Deane	18/12/14	
Lieut.	Frielinghaus, Arthur	1/12/14	Awarded, Italian Silver Medal, *Lon. Gaz.*, 31/8/17. Mentioned in despatches, *Lon. Gaz.*, 20/6/17.
Lieut.	Frielinghaus, Heinrick Oloff	1/12/14	
Lieut.	Graham, Mungo Alan	21/11/14	
Lieut.	Griffiths, Albert William Madoc	5/12/14	Died.
Lieut.	Harris, D.S.O., Frank Ernest	30/11/14	Mentioned in despatches, *Lon. Gaz.*, 8/2/17.
Lieut.	MacKenzie, Frederick Percy	17/11/14	Wounded, 12/2/16.
Lieut.	Mitchell, Mortimer Alfred	8/1/15	
Lieut.	Neville, Ralph Ewing	18/9/15	
Lieut.	Nicol, William Benjamin	7/11/14	Wounded, 30/5/16.
Lieut.	Prew, Harold Edward	9/1/15	Killed, 1/8/17.
Lieut.	Rabone, Philip	14/11/14	
Lieut.	Robertson, William Cleland	31/8/15	
Lieut.	Usher, Thomas Nicholas Joseph	24/11/14	
1321 Pte.	Abegglen, Alfred	4/8/15	
908 Pte.	Aberdeen, John Young	14/12/14	
1246 Pte.	Ackermann, Andries Johannes	6/9/15	Wounded, 11/3/16. Died.
1360 Pte.	Acton, Lloyd Edward	7/9/15	
978 Pte.	Adams, Alexander Maxwell	16/12/15	
773 Sgt.	Addicott, Thomas George	27/11/14	Wounded, 2/6/16.
650 L/Sgt.	Adkins, Reginald Stapleton	10/11/14	Died.
681 Pte.	Airth, George	17/11/14	
1574 Pte.	Alcock, Frank	14/3/16	Died.
1446 Pte.	Alexander, John Graham	29/9/15	
662 Pte.	Alexander, Victor Charles	12/11/14	Killed, 17/8/16.
1069 Pte.	Allen, Frank	12/1/15	
528 Pte.	Allen, Thomas	29/10/14	

IN EAST AFRICA

			Attested.	
830	Cpl.	Allen, Frank Sydney	26/11/14	Died, Salisbury 11/9/17.
1047	Pte.	Allman, Edwin James	11/1/15	
822	Pte.	Anderson, Carl Gustave Frederick	25/11/14	
641	Pte.	Anderson, Charles Scott	7/11/14	
1596	Pte.	Anderson, Ernest Fletcher	9/4/16	
639	Pte.	Anderson, Thomas William	7/11/14	
1207	Pte.	Andreasen, Peter	30/8/15	Killed, 11/3/16.
831	Pte.	Andrews, James Merry	30/11/14	
725	Pte.	Anfield, Cecil Henry	13/11/14	
1312	Pte.	Archdall, Edgar St. Clair	28/8/15	Wounded, 11/3/16.
760	Col/Sgt.	Armitage, Frederick Arthur	24/11/14	
1347	Pte.	Arnott, Henry	14/9/15	
767	Pte.	Ashburner, Roland	26/11/14	Wounded, 11/3/15.
1144	Pte.	Athiendes, Gabriel Paul	16/8/15	
1223	Pte.	Badham, Philip James	6/9/15	Wounded, 17/8/16
592	Pte.	Bain, Herbert	2/11/14	
1542	Pte.	Bain, Michael Edward	7/2/16	
1351	Cpl.	Baines, Charles Wyndham Quinn	14/9/15	
1096	Pte.	Baker, George	17/7/15	
1172	L/Cpl.	Ballam, Ernest William	21/8/15	Wounded, 2/6/16.
1127	L/Sgt.	Ballinger, D.C.M., William Henry	7/8/15	Wounded, 11/3/16. Awarded D.C.M., *Lon. Gaz.*, 27/7/16. Awarded St. George's Cross, *Lon. Gaz.*, 15/2/17. Mentioned in despatches *Lon. Gaz.*, 8/2/17.
494	L/Cpl.	Banner, John William	27/10/14	Died.
1363	Pte.	Baragwanath, Thomas Vyvyan	14/8/15	
1027	Pte.	Barber, Charles Thomas	8/1/15	
824	L/Cpl.	Bateman, Gladstone	26/11/14	Died.
327	Sgt.	Bates, Lewis	23/10/14	Killed, 12/3/16.
1516	Pte.	Battersby, James McKeand	6/1/16	
1478	Pte.	Baxter, Edward	30/10/15	
1364	Pte.	Baxter, Harry	7/9/15	Died.
1089	Pte.	Bayliffe, Leonard Frederick	25/1/15	Wounded, 11/3/16. Mentioned in despatches, *Lon. Gaz.*, 30/1/17.

THE 2ND RHODESIA REGIMENT

			Attested.	
872	L/Cpl.	Beale, Frank Edward	17/12/14	
1113	Pte.	Beaufort, Percy Mostyn	31/7/15	
883	L/Cpl.	Beck, Edgar Hudson	22/12/14	
1510	Pte.	Becker, Denis	20/12/15	Died, Niarobi, 7/5/16.
686	Pte.	Becker, Reginald Wren	18/11/14	
1619	Pte.	Bekker, Martinus Johannes	18/5/16	
1429	Pte.	Bell, Frank	18/9/15	
961	Pte.	Bellair, Richard	22/1/15	
1248	Pte.	Benford, Edward John	28/8/15	
819	Pte.	Bennett, Charles Hector	25/11/14	
1500	Pte.	Bennett, Malcolm Thomas	2/12/15	
820	Pte.	Bennett, William Edward	25/11/14	Killed, 11/3/16.
813	Pte.	Bennett, William Henry	24/11/14	
1639	Pte.	Berrington, Arthur Street	21/7/16	Died.
1640	Pte.	Berrington, Eric William Colin	21/7/16	
1301	Pte.	Bindiman, Ferdinand	27/8/15	
1614	Pte.	Birkin, Melville Essex	5/5/16	
1362	L/Cpl.	Blackhall, James	8/9/15	
804	Pte.	Blair, George Swan	21/11/14	Wounded, 12/3/16.
1595	Pte.	Blair, Robert Simpson	10/4/16	
1332	Cpl.	Blake, Alfred Henry	30/8/15	
1119	Pte.	Blake, John Norman	4/8/15	
912	Pte.	Blamey, William	18/1/15	Died, Voi, 20/6/15.
1018	Pte.	Blue, Percy	5/1/15	
1093	Pte.	Blurton, Rupert Oliver Hardy	10/7/15	
1171	Cpl.	Boddington, Charles	21/8/15	Wounded, 12/2/16.
988	Pte.	Bolus, Gerald Warren	25/2/15	Killed, 12/3/16.
1058	Pte.	Boncey, Frederick	12/1/15	
643	Cpl.	Bosworth, James Allen	9/11/14	
1236	Pte.	Botes, Anthonia Johannes	9/9/15	Wounded, 12/3/16.
1368	Pte.	Botha, Barand Ben	4/9/15	
560	Sgt.	Botha, Rumbald Gregorowski	29/10/14	
566	Pte.	Bott, Joseph	30/10/14	
741	Pte.	Bower, Ernest	20/11/14	
1366	Pte.	Bowie, George	9/9/15	
1682	Pte.	Bowley, Garnet Victor	10/11/16	
937	L/Cpl.	Boyd, David	9/1/15	
947	Pte.	Bradshaw, Alexander John	13/1/15	
867	Pte.	Brailsford, Henry Edward Law	6/12/14	
1307	Pte.	Brand, John Baxter	30/8/15	
627	Sgt.	Braund, Joseph Beadwell	6/11/14	

			Attested.	
711	Sgt.	Brazier, Charles Valentine	9/11/14	
777	Pte.	Brazier, Edwin	1/12/14	
862	Pte.	Breach, Basil Ingram	11/12/14	
1454	Pte.	Breedt, Jacobus Johannes	5/10/15	
571	Pte.	Brent, Jonathan	31/10/14	
430	Pte.	Brereton, Frank Sadler	24/10/14	
1297	Pte.	Brimacombe, John	8/9/15	
832	Pte.	Broadbent, David	30/11/14	
435	Sgt.	Brodie, Patrick Tait	26/10/14	
1032	Cpl.	Brokensha, Thomas William	8/1/15	
881	Pte.	Brooks, Melville Hoaten	21/12/14	
629	Q.M.S.	Broom, John Frost	6/11/14	
720	Pte.	Brothwell, William Frederick	11/11/14	
995	Sgt.	Brown, Louis Maurice	5/3/15	
1367	Pte.	Brown, Robert Norman	9/9/15	
1450	Pte.	Brown, William Clement	2/10/15	Wounded, 11/3/16.
982	L/Sgt.	Bruce, David	18/2/18	
821	Pte.	Brummitt, James	23/11/14	
1300	Pte.	Bruton, Frederick Donald	31/8/15	
698	Pte.	Bryce, David	19/11/14	Wounded, 5/6/15 and 11/3/16.
1196	Pte.	Buchanan, James	27/8/15	Wounded, 12/3/16. Died.
1645	Pte.	Buckle, Barend Frederick	27/7/16	
1644	Pte.	Buckle, Thomas	27/7/16	
1617	Pte.	Buckley, Henry John	13/5/16	
1181	Pte.	Burdett, Edward Fiennes	25/8/15	Wounded, 30/5/16.
1108	Pte.	Burkitt, William Kendrick	28/7/15	
964	Pte.	Burt, Ernest	28/1/15	
762	Pte.	Bush, Edward George White	24/11/14	
1328	Cpl.	Calder, John	7/9/15	
1642	Pte.	Caldcott, Walter	24/7/16	
1612	Pte.	Cameron, Jack	4/5/16	
475	Sgt.	Cameron, Robert Rose	24/10/14	Died.
603	Pte.	Campbell, Charles Christopher	3/11/14	
1147	Pte.	Campbell, Douglas Henry	17/8/15	
996	Pte.	Carisson, John	6/5/15	
1087	Sgt.	Carter, Arthur Roland	19/1/15	Killed, 12/2/16.

			Attested.	
1235	Pte.	Cashel, Edward Charles Baldwin	9/9/15	Wounded, 17/8/16.
887	Cpl.	Catchpole, Ernest Keithby	24/12/14	
640	Pte.	Cato, Jack	7/11/14	
724	Pte.	Cawood, Martin David	13/11/14	
1646	Pte.	Celliers, Sarel Jacobus	27/7/16	
595	Pte.	Chaddock, John	2/11/14	
1284	Sgt.	Chadwick, Reginald Martin	27/8/15	Died.
994	Pte.	Chadwick, William	5/3/15	
785	L/Sgt.	Chalmers, Hudson Pullen	1/12/14	
744	L/Cpl.	Chalmers, Robert Gerald	21/11/14	
1629	Pte.	Chamberlain, Walter Birrell	14/6/16	
1094	Pte.	Chambers, Raymond	12/7/15	
1249	Pte.	Chambers, Walter John	30/8/15	
1447	Pte.	Chapman, Ernest Alfred	29/9/15	
1475	Pte.	Charters, D.C.M., Alfred Graham	28/10/15	
929	L/Cpl.	Charton, M.C., Godfrey	4/1/15	
735	Pte.	Chave, John	18/11/14	Killed, 13/5/15.
1165	Cpl.	Christie, Albert William	20/8/15	
1560	Pte.	Cinnamon, Alexander	29/2/16	
811	L/Cpl.	Clack, Harold Gilbert	23/11/14	
835	L/Cpl.	Clark, Frederick	28/11/14	Died.
1292	Pte.	Clark, Henry Alfred	14/8/15	
700	Cpl.	Clark, Reginald Stanley	7/11/14	
840	Pte.	Clark, Wilfred John Bedwel	30/11/14	
1474	Pte.	Clark, William	20/10/15	
1607	Pte.	Clarke, Frederick Allison	26/4/16	
1527	Pte.	Clarke, George Edmund	17/1/16	
1526	Pte.	Clarke, John William	17/1/16	Wounded, 12/3/16.
1371	Pte.	Clay, Charles Henry	2/9/15	
653	Cpl.	Clipstone, William	11/11/14	
1219	Sgt.	Cloete, Albert Ernest	2/9/15	
730	Pte.	Cock, Clifford	16/11/14	Wounded, 30/5/16.
1124	Pte.	Coetzee, Cornelius Lawrence	7/8/15	
1369	Cpl.	Cohen, Bertram	9/9/15	
607	Pte.	Coles, Sydney	3/11/14	
903	L/Cpl.	Coley, Douglas	12/12/14	
1504	Pte.	Colley, James	7/12/15	Wounded, 17/8/16.

IN EAST AFRICA 109

Attested.

1616	Pte.	Collins, Victor Henry	9/5/16	
958	L/Cpl.	Collins, Vincent Henry	14/1/15	Died.
684	L/Cpl.	Cook, Albert Whiteley	18/11/14	
644	L/Cpl.	Cookson, John	9/11/14	
601	L/Cpl.	Cooper, Augustus Bordman	3/11/14	
731	Pte.	Cormack, Alexander	16/11/14	Died, Wynberg, 14/2/17.
833	Pte.	Corrick, Ernest	1/12/14	
997	Pte.	Couper, James	6/3/15	Died.
764	Pte.	Coutts, Walter Taylor	24/11/14	
1487	Pte.	Cowan, Frederick Thomas	15/11/15	
913	Pte.	Cowell, Herbert Henry	22/12/14	
1233	Pte.	Cowie, John Andrew	8/9/15	
1229	Pte.	Cox, Russell Ian	8/9/15	
816	Pte.	Cox, Vincent Hitchinson	24/11/14	Killed, 17/8/16.
984	Pte.	Coxwell, George Louth	22/2/15	
974	Pte.	Coxwell, William Stewart Gordon	13/2/15	Wounded, 17/8/16. Died.
1507	Pte.	Craig, Robert	11/12/15	Wounded, 11/3/16.
1091	Sgt.	Cranswick, Gerald Hope	9/7/15	
1601	Pte.	Cromer, John Henry	19/4/16	
1597	Pte.	Cripps, Harold	11/4/16	
1169	Sgt.	Cripps, Lionel John	20/8/15	
1666	Pte.	Croft, John Daniel	1/10/16	
718	Cpl.	Crook, Frederick Dennis	10/11/14	Wounded, 14/7/15.
1063	Pte.	Crossland, Alfred	12/1/15	Died, 23/9/16, Karonque.
1676	Pte.	Crouch, Frederick	26/10/16	
1502	Pte.	Cruse, Sidney Benjamin	4/12/15	
1160	Pte.	Cullen, Archibald	27/8/15	
918	Pte.	Culley, Harvey Redfern	29/12/14	
1350	Pte.	Cumming, James Arthur Maldwin	14/9/15	
1370	Pte.	Curran, Peter	9/9/15	
1518	Pte.	Currie, Alexander	6/1/16	
945	Pte.	Curtis, Reginald Francis Scaer	11/1/15	
799	Pte.	Cuthbert, Albert James	7/12/14	Died.
1379	Pte.	Daly, Roland Charles Gordon	6/9/15	
875	Pte.	Darby, Herbert	17/12/14	
1055	Pte.	Darley, Herbert Ivon	12/1/15	
1611	Pte.	Davey, Horace William	28/4/16	

			Attested.	
1098	Pte.	Davies, Clifford Hamilton Brown	19/7/15	
1182	Cpl.	Davies, David Walter	24/8/15	
1190	Pte.	Davies, Ernest	25/8/15	
1589	Pte.	Davies, Jeffries Lee	5/4/16	
1679	Pte.	Davies, Leo Edwin	3/11/16	
715	Pte.	Davies, Ronald Mitford	9/12/14	
1150	Pte.	Davies, Ronald Ralph	18/8/15	
1117	Pte.	Davies, Stewart Gwynne	29/7/15	
983	Cpl.	Davies, Thomas Emlyn	18/2/15	
1608	Pte.	Davies, Thomas Rees	26/4/16	Wounded, 17/8/16
1273	Cpl.	Davies, Walter	31/8/15	
1330	Pte.	Dawson, James	25/8/15	
774	Pte.	Day, Charles Warren	29/11/14	
1592	Pte.	Day, Henry Welsted	7/4/16	
1138	Pte.	Day, John Brampton	21/8/15	
1238	Pte.	Deacon, William Charles Edward	9/9/15	
647	Pte.	De Beer, Jack Eric	9/11/14	
1102	Pte.	De Buys, Albert John Philip	23/7/15	
465	Pte.	De Lautour, Cecil Andrew	26/10/14	Died, 4/11/15.
1382	Pte.	Dempster, David	6/9/15	
888	Pte.	Denn, John Adam	26/12/14	
565	Pte.	Dennis, John Francis Dugdale	30/10/14	
1378	Pte.	De Pierres, Joseph William	9/9/15	
530	Pte.	Derbyshire, Henry	29/10/14	
1280	Pte.	De Reuck, John Peter	3/9/15	
1381	Pte.	Devenish, George Walter	8/9/15	
415	Sgt.	Devitt, Herbert John	24/10/14	Died.
690	Sgt.	Dewar, Hugh McPherson	19/11/14	
1318	Pte.	Diack, William	31/8/15	
790	Pte.	Dick, Andrew Campbell	1/12/14	Died.
710	L/Cpl.	Dick, Archibald Gemmel	9/11/14	
1380	Pte.	Dicks, Ivon Bernard	7/9/15	
1383	Pte.	Dickson, John Morrison	7/9/15	
1126	Pte.	Dissel, Hubert	7/8/15	
876	Pte.	Dixon, Frank	18/12/14	
1566	Pte.	Dodds, Arthur Douglas	4/3/16	
1376	Pte.	Doherty, Mathew	10/9/15	Wounded, 12/3/16.
420	Pte.	Donaldson, William	24/10/14	
470	Sgt.	Donkin, William	27/10/14	

IN EAST AFRICA

			Attested.	
1049	Sgt.	Dorehill, William John	11/1/15	
1088	L/Cpl.	Douglas, Allan	25/1/15	
1009	L/Cpl.	Douglas, Stewart James	2/1/15	
1377	Pte.	Dowdney, Alfred	10/9/15	
920	Pte.	Doyle, Alfred Thomas	29/12/14	Killed, 9/6/16.
1372	Pte.	Doyle, John Henry	31/8/15	
1290	Cpl.	Dreyer, Francis Robert Bromley	31/8/15	
1374	Pte.	Driver, Richard Francis	9/9/15	
1587	Pte.	Duglan, William Henry	2/4/16	
1054	Pte.	Durrant, William Short	12/1/15	
1513	Pte.	Dwyer, Joseph	5/1/16	
492	Pte.	Eades, Henry Gordon	27/10/14	
1672	Pte.	Eadie, William	14/10/16	
1180	Pte.	Earnshaw, John	23/8/15	Died.
1023	Pte.	Eastwood, George Marmaduke	7/1/15	
1434	Pte.	Eastwood, Harold Gordon	21/9/15	Wounded, 12/3/16.
1624	Sgt.	Edkins, John	29/5/16	Mentioned in despatches, Lon. Gaz., 2/8/18.
761	Cpl.	Edwards, Alfred Toms	24/11/14	
1662	Pte.	Edwards, Arthur	17/9/16	
782	Pte.	Edwards, Nathaniel	1/12/14	Died, Morogoro, 5/2/17.
935	L/Cpl.	Edwards, Walter	8/1/15	
1358	Pte.	Ekstein, John Hendrick	16/9/15	
1216	Pte.	Ellis, Patrick Henry	1/9/15	
1599	Pte.	Elsworth, John Campbell	15/4/16	
1237	Pte.	Elton, Corbett Henry	9/9/15	
521	Pte.	Ely, Thomas	29/10/14	Killed, 11/3/16.
1385	Pte.	Emms, Leslie Lilliwhite	6/9/15	
1121	Pte.	English, John Morris	4/8/15	
1508	Pte.	Enright, Frank	11/9/17	
1327	Pte.	Erasmus, Gert Martinus	26/8/15	
726	Pte.	Erasmus, Peter Rasmus	13/11/14	
1641	Pte.	Esterhuizen, Joseph	24/7/16	
1442	Pte.	Evans, M.C., D.C.M., Harold Charles De Courcy	28/9/15	Awarded, D.C.M., Lon. Gaz., 31/5/16. St. George's Cross, Lon. Gaz., 15/2/17. Mentioned in despatches, Lon. Gaz., 8/2/17.
1637	Pte.	Eyles, Eric Wolfgang	14/7/16	

			Attested.	
787	Pte.	Faber, Otto	1/12/14	Killed, 8/5/15.
1070	Pte.	Fairbrother, Frederick Charles	15/1/15	
1299	L/Sgt.	Faulkner, Frederick Joseph	30/8/15	Died, 19/1/17.
1232	Pte.	Fensom, Arthur Abraham	8/9/15	
732	Pte.	Fereday, Harry Stanley	16/11/14	
734	Pte.	Ferguson, Claude Henry	17/11/14	
1576	Pte.	Ferguson, Thomas Andrew	26/3/16	
1005	Pte.	Ferguson, William	2/1/15	
1231	Pte.	Ferriera, Luke Martinus	8/9/15	
854	Pte.	Fiander, Charles Eric Graham Reid	9/12/14	Died, 4/8/16.
1559	Pte.	Fiander, Lionel Evan	29/2/16	Wounded, 7/8/16.
789	Pte.	Finaughty, Fleming	1/12/14	
1337	Pte.	Finch, John	1/9/15	
1341	Pte.	Findlater, Charles	30/8/15	
1186	Pte.	Fish, Richard	25/8/15	Died.
694	Sgt.	Fisher, Arnold Alexander Giles	19/11/14	
933	Pte.	Fisher, Richard John	7/1/15	
1034	Sgt.	Flaxman, Thomas	8/1/15	
959	Pte.	Flugge, Max	21/1/15	
1250	L/Cpl.	Ford, Alfred Marshall	4/9/15	
1578	Pte.	Foreman, Cecil Markham	28/3/16	
1201	Pte.	Fouchee, Adrian Isaac	28/8/15	
652	Pte.	Fountain, Geoffrey	11/11/14	
673	Pte.	Francis, Frederick Falconer	14/11/14	
486	Pte.	Franken, Peter Jeffrey	27/10/14	
1457	Pte.	Fraser, Charles Winton	8/10/15	Killed, 11/3/16.
1550	Pte.	Frost, John Wesley	9/2/16	
893	Pte.	Frost, Thomas Lauder	29/12/14	
874	Cpl.	Fuller, Douglas	17/12/14	
613	Pte.	Fuller, Frank Edward	4/11/14	Died.
986	Sgt.	Fuller, George Philip	24/2/15	
1043	L/Sgt.	Furmston, Edward Thomas	7/1/15	
791	Pte.	Furse, Frederick Charles Lewis	1/12/14	
626	Pte.	Fynn, Bernard Cotrell Holmes	24/10/14	Died.
575	Pte.	Gale, Leopold Allen	31/10/14	
942	Pte.	Callagher, Charles	9/1/15	
771	L/Cpl.	Gallagher, Patrick	17/11/14	Wounded, 17/8/16.
971	Pte.	Gammis, William Lawrence	6/2/15	
1635	Pte.	Gammon, Frank Joseph	1/7/16	

IN EAST AFRICA 113

			Attested.	
1116	Pte.	Garland, Percival Randall	28/7/15	
860	Pte.	Gaunt, Robert Peddie	14/12/14	
1217	Pte.	Geitzmann, John William	1/9/15	
1304	Pte.	Geoghegan, Charles Augustus	30/8/15	
1298	Cpl.	Geraty, Donald Stewart	26/8/15	
1390	Pte.	Gibbs, Edward Victor Rees	9/9/15	
1388	Pte.	Gibbs, Jack	6/9/15	
1259	Pte.	Gibson, James Alfred	31/8/15	
1389	Pte.	Giels, Alexander Elmsley	8/9/15	
1159	Pte.	Gietzmann, Bernard Andrew William	18/8/15	
1228	Pte.	Gilbert, William Henry	8/9/15	
680	Cpl.	Gillespie, David Young	17/11/14	
1561	Pte.	Gillett, Horace	29/2/16	
1295	Pte.	Gilliland, John Knox	1/9/15	
1324	Pte.	Gleave, John	2/9/15	
1114	Pte.	Godbolt, Clarence Burleigh	2/8/15	
963	Pte.	Goddard, Alfred Percy	27/1/15	
733	Cpl.	Going, Carl Henry Bernard	17/11/14	Died.
1178	Pte.	Going, Francis Hardinge	23/8/15	
1317	Pte.	Gordon, Thomas Spencer	30/8/15	
990	Pte.	Goudie, Arnold James	4/3/15	Wounded, 12/3/16. Died.
1638	Pte.	Gould, Harry	17/7/16	Died.
946	Sgt.	Gould, Henry Edward	18/8/15	
1130	Pte.	Goulding, William Stanley	10/8/15	
1154	Pte.	Gowan, Andrew Grant	18/8/15	
1455	Pte.	Gowing, Hubert James	7/10/15	Died.
617	Pte.	Graham, George	4/11/14	
852	Pte.	Grant, Angus	8/12/14	Died.
1553	Pte.	Grant, John	15/2/16	
1135	Pte.	Grant, John Duncan	6/8/15	
976	Pte.	Grant, Walter	13/2/15	
1623	Pte.	Grant, William Bland	23/5/16	Died.
1026	Pte.	Graves, Harry	4/1/15	
1226	Pte.	Greaves, Charles	8/9/15	
1495	Pte.	Gregory, Henry John	20/11/15	
850	Pte.	Green, Arthur Graham	7/12/14	Died, Voi, 7/4/16.
633	C9l/Sgt.	Green, George D.C.M.,	6/11/14	Awarded, D.C.M., *Lon. Gaz.*, 27/7/17. Awarded St. George's Cross, *Lon. Gaz.*, 15/2/17. Mentioned in despatches 8/3/17.

G

THE 2ND RHODESIA REGIMENT

Attested.

No.	Rank	Name	Date	Notes
1659	Pte.	Grey, Alexander	10/9/16	
1105	Pte.	Grove, John Edward	27/7/15	
1006	L/Cpl.	Guiney, Arthur Wilson	4/1/15	Mentioned in despatches, *Lon. Gaz.*, 30/6/17. Died.
1591	Cpl.	Hacking, Ernest John	7/4/16	
1014	Pte.	Hacking, Harry Walter	5/1/15	
1484	Pte.	Hagan, John	12/11/15	
1480	Pte.	Hageman, Julius Charles	3/11/15	
1056	Sgt.	Hall, James Edward	12/1/15	Died.
1242	Pte.	Hall, William	9/9/15	
1187	Pte.	Halliday, Charles	25/8/15	
1391	Pte.	Halliwell, Robert Darrell	7/9/15	
1583	Pte.	Halls, Herbert John	1/4/16	
927	L/Cpl.	Hamilton, John	2/1/15	Died, 26/7/15.
1084	Pte.	Hamling, Hubert Hamlyn	19/1/15	
1392	Pte.	Hargrave, Green	11/9/15	
1251	Pte.	Harrington, Peter	7/9/15	
1467	Pte.	Harris, Samuel Henry	11/10/15	
1634	Pte.	Harrower, Alexander Peter Nicol	26/6/16	
1257	Pte.	Hart, Austin Vernon	14/8/15	
973	L/Cpl.	Hart, Charles Ambrose	13/2/15	Awarded, Medaille Militaire, *Lon. Gaz.*, 31/8/17. Mentioned in despatches, *Lon. Gaz.*, 8/2/17. Died.
1468	Pte.	Harvey, William Oldnall	12/10/15	
1571	Pte.	Haselwood, Clarence	14/3/16	
677	Pte.	Haslam, Andrew	17/11/14	Wounded, 12/3/16.
1191	Pte.	Haslam, John	25/8/15	
1663	Pte.	Hastings, Richard	22/9/16	
1667	Pte.	Havell, William Henry	1/10/16	
1293	Pte.	Havenga, Johannes Jacobus	31/8/15	
1534	Pte.	Havner, William Jackson	27/1/16	Died.
1197	Pte.	Hawkins, George	27/8/15	
858	Pte.	Hay, John	12/12/14	Died.
1393	Pte.	Hazlett, Robert Ernest	9/9/15	
611	Pte.	Heath, Walter Charles	4/11/14	Died.
1120	Pte.	Heck, Frederick William	4/8/15	
1279	Pte.	Hendry, Ronald Charles	26/8/15	
848	Pte.	Henry, Travers Helmore	3/12/14	
1313	Pte.	Herbert, Percy Albert	30/8/15	
1156	Pte.	Herbst, Johann Francois	18/8/15	
1155	Pte.	Herbst, William Seigfried	18/8/15	
1252	Pte.	Heugh, Leander Van Reenen	3/9/15	

			Attested.	
532	Pte.	Hewett, Frank	29/10/14	
1067	Pte.	Hick, Edward	14/1/15	
1309	Pte.	Hickey, William	30/8/15	
1319	Pte.	Higgins, Harold Andrew	16/8/15	Died, 19/10/17.
1355	Pte.	Higgs, Sidney Bone	15/9/15	Died.
808	Pte.	Higgs, William George	22/11/14	
1253	Pte.	Hill, Herbert Edward	6/9/15	Wounded, 12/3/16.
1205	L/Cpl.	Hill, William Robertson	30/8/15	
1565	Pte.	Hipwell, M.M., Henry Havilock	5/3/16	Died.
864	Col/Sgt.	Hodgkin, Sydney Thomas	14/12/14	Died.
914	Pte.	Hodgson, Charles	23/12/14	
588	Pte.	Hodson, James Jeffries	2/11/14	
1564	Pte.	Hodson, Trevor	7/3/16	
1627	Pte.	Holder, Frederick Charles	5/6/16	
414	C.S.M.	Holland, Rupert Stafford Ayre	24/10/14	
563	Col/Sgt.	Holmes, D.C.M., Bertram Medd	30/10/14	Awarded D.C.M., *Lon. Gaz.*, 3/3/17. Mentioned in despatches, *Lon. Gaz.*, 8/2/17. Died.
1083	Pte.	Holmes, Norman Clifford	16/1/15	
1352	Pte.	Holmes, Robert Wilson	14/9/15	Killed, 11/3/16.
1046	Pte.	Holohan, Charles Justin	11/1/15	
1199	Pte.	Homan, Digby Arden	28/8/15	Killed, 12/3/16.
977	L/Cpl.	Honey, Conrad Stanford	13/2/15	
1626	Pte.	Hope, Francis	2/6/16	
868	L/Cpl.	Hopkins, John Gerald	14/12/14	
1661	Pte.	Hornby, Arthur	13/9/16	
1103	Pte.	Horne, William	26/7/15	
1683	Pte.	Howard, Robert	15/11/16	
1359	Pte.	Howard, William	16/9/15	
1439	Pte.	Howe, Harry Jarvis	27/9/15	Killed, 11/3/16.
1142	Sgt.	Hubie, Sydney Rylands	16/8/15	Died.
899	Cpl.	Hudson, Robert	30/12/14	Died
589	Pte.	Huggins, Philip Michael	2/11/14	
590	Cpl.	Huggins, Reuben Hugh	2/11/14	Died.
1145	Pte.	Hughes, Edward	17/8/15	Died.
671	Sgt.	Hughes, Owen Prys	14/11/14	
1213	Pte.	Hulley, Cecil Malcolm	31/8/15	
1543	Pte.	Hulley, Clement Richard	7/2/16	
979	Pte.	Hunt, Aubrey William	16/2/15	
1019	Pte.	Hunt, Harry Travers	5/1/15	

THE 2ND RHODESIA REGIMENT

Attested.

587	Pte.	Hunter, William Alan	2/11/14	
1224	Sgt.	Hunter, William MacPherson	6/9/15	
1060	L/Sgt.	Hurr, Edward Brown	13/1/15	Died, 13/4/16.
1658	Pte.	Hussey, Joseph	31/8/16	
683	Sgt.	Hutcheon, Albert Ernest	17/11/14	
1262	Pte.	Hutchings, Bethel	3/9/15	
1563	Pte.	Huxtable, Lionel Taylor	3/3/16	
968	Pte.	Idle, Charles	4/2/15	
879	Pte.	Inskipp, Norman	21/12/14	
1613	Pte.	Jackson, Alfred Oswald	3/5/16	
1490	Pte.	Jackson, Chester Francis	17/11/15	
1498	Pte.	Jackson, Ernest Gordon	1/12/15	
697	Pte.	James, Charles Edward	19/11/14	
1212	Pte.	Jamieson, Robert Gran	1/9/15	Killed, 12/2/16.
1029	Pte.	Jarman, Bernard	8/1/15.	
962	Cpl.	Jarvis, Henry John	27/1/15	
1488	Pte.	Jasper, William	15/11/15	Wounded, 17/8/16.
829	Pte.	Jeffreys, Charles Magnus James	28/11/14	
1208	Pte.	Jelliman, Llewellyn Pollard	30/8/15	
792	Sgt.	Jenkins, William Llewellyn	2/12/14	Wounded, 12/3/16.
522	Pte.	Jenkinson, Harry	20/10/14	Died.
1528	Pte.	Jennison, Frederick Charles	20/1/16	
709	Cpl.	Johansen, D.C.M., August Louis	9/11/14	Awarded D.C.M., (prompt award), 22/8/17.
657	Pte.	Johnson, Sydney Edward	20/10/14	
1082	Pte.	Johnstone, George Frederick	16/1/15	
1625	Pte.	Johnstone, James Arthur	2/6/16	Died.
1349	Pte.	Johnstone, Reginald Henry	14/9/15	Killed, 11/3/16.
1081	Pte.	Johnstone, Walter Peter	16/1/15	
1344	Pte.	Jones, Allen Rutherfoord	13/9/15	
1195	Pte.	Jones, James Lloyd	26/8/15	
987	Pte.	Jones, John	25/2/15	
1289	Cpl.	Jones, Laurence	31/8/15	
707	Sgt.	Jones, Samuel	8/11/14	
142	Pte.	Jones, Stanley Boscawen	20/10/14	

IN EAST AFRICA

			Attested.	
1579	Pte.	Jones, William Martell	31/3/16	
666	L/Cpl.	Jones, William Runcroft	14/11/14	
1062	Pte.	Jordan, Alfred Perkins	12/1/15	
1100	Pte.	Joss, George Stewart	21/7/15	
1469	Pte.	Jowett, Leonard Victor	13/10/15	
1394	Pte.	Jury, George	7/8/17	
948	Pte.	Keen, Leonard George William	13/1/15	
71	Sgt.	Kekewich, George Edward	22/10/14	
1656	Pte.	Kelleher, John Joseph	28/8/16	Died.
596	L/Cpl.	Kelly, John William	2/11/14	
776	Pte.	Kelly, Montague William	30/11/14	
651	Pte.	Kelly, Oswald Claude	10/11/14	
894	Pte.	Kelly, Percy Dennis	29/12/14	Killed, 11/3/16.
936	Pte.	Kelly, Thomas William Alfred	9/1/15	
1296	Pte.	Kemp, Sutherland Ronald	1/9/15	Wounded, 12/3/16.
1460	Pte.	Kennedy, Allan	16/9/15	Died.
926	Pte.	Kennedy, Patrick	28/12/14	
1132	Pte.	Kerr, Lance Ivor	11/8/15	Wounded, 12/3/16.
1112	Pte.	Killen, Claude Keir Murray	30/7/15	
750	Pte.	Killen, Graham Desmond	22/11/14	
1007	L/Cpl.	Kimber, Frank	4/1/15	Died.
1431	Pte.	King, Alfred	20/9/15	
1643	Pte.	King, Allan Edwig Macfarlane	25/7/16	
1086	Cpl.	King, David Melville	19/1/15	Died.
1584	Pte.	Kinnear, Robert Taylor	1/4/16	
531	Col/Sgt.	Kirby, Harry	29/10/14	
1501	Pte.	Kirkwood, Charles	2/12/14	
1525	Pte.	Knowles, William	16/1/16	
1016	Pte.	Knutzen, Lief Murer	4/1/15	
1586	Pte.	Koch, Daniel Turner	3/4/16	
1395	Pte.	Koch, Julius	8/9/15	
1548	Pte.	Koen, Charles Michael	9/2/16	Died, Salisbury, 18/2/17.
756	Pte.	Koning, John Henry	24/11/14	
620	Pte.	Krienke, Reuben	4/11/14	
1254	Pte.	Kruger, William Jacobus	31/8/15	Wounded, 12/3/16.
1433	Pte.	Kuys, Alexander Maurice	21/9/15	

			Attested.	
203	Pte.	Lamprecht, Andries Jacobus	20/10/14	
585	Pte.	Lang, William Albert	2/11/14	
1203	Pte.	Lawrence, Andrew	28/8/15	
1274	Pte.	Lawson, John	30/8/15	
1648	Pte.	Lawrence, Valentine Alexander	5/8/16	
966	L/Sgt.	Ledingham, Alfred John	4/2/15	
1033	L/Cpl.	Lee, Owen Vincent	8/1/15	
1230	Pte.	Legattie, Bennie	8/9/15	
614	Pte.	LeGrange, Henry Lewis	4/11/14	
1470	Pte.	Le Roux, Dirk Cornelius	20/9/15	
1163	L/Cpl.	Leslie, George Louis	19/8/15	
981	Pte.	Levet, William	17/2/15	
682	Sgt.	Levet, Cyril	17/11/14	
691	Pte.	Levy, Harry	9/11/14	
1396	Pte.	Lewin, William	8/9/15	
1472	Pte.	Lewis, William Francis	15/10/15	
1200	Pte.	Liddle, Edward Lothian	28/8/15	
1445	Pte.	Liddle, John Lothian	29/9/15	
1398	Pte.	Liesching, Frederick Louis	6/9/15	Died.
1580	Pte.	Liggins, Joseph Frank	30/3/16	
545	Pte.	Lister, Alfred	30/10/14	
772	Sgt.	Littlefair, Charles Septimus	27/11/14	
1609	Pte.	Littlewood, Henry	28/4/16	
57	Pte.	Lloyd, Arthur Wilfred	21/10/14	
580	Sgt.	Lock, Edward Percy	2/11/14	
1554	Pte.	Long, George	16/2/16	
1664	Pte.	Long, Leslie Maitland	28/9/16	
1333	Pte.	Lorensen, Leendert	27/8/15	
907	Pte.	Lott, Percy Emmanuel	14/12/14	
897	Pte.	Louw, Peter Jacobus	30/12/14	
1577	Pte.	Lowe, Frank Harold	26/3/16	
1335	Pte.	Lowe, George Edward	6/9/15	
1011	Pte.	Lowenshaw, Michael	5/1/15	Wounded, 12/3/16.
1218	Pte.	Lucas, Hector James	1/9/15	
1494	Pte.	Lunn, Gordon Passmore	22/11/15	
1101	Pte.	Lurie, Isaac	22/7/15	
1397	Sgt.	Lyons, George Alfred	10/9/15	
931	Pte.	Lyons, Robert James Peter	7/1/15	Wounded, 9/6/16.
938	Pte.	MacDonald, Alexander	9/1/15	
1615	Pte.	MacDonald, John Archie	6/5/16	Died, 22/8/16.
1151	Pte.	MacDonald, Peter	18/8/15	

IN EAST AFRICA

			Attested.	
1030	Pte.	MacHugh, John James	8/1/15	
1079	Pte.	MacKay, William Henry	16/1/15	
1177	Cpl.	MacKenzie, Francis Archer	23/8/15	
1506	L/Cpl.	MacKinnon, Donald William Henry	8/12/15	
1403	Pte.	MacKintosh, Harry Forbes	6/9/15	Wounded, 30/5/16. Died.
1499	Pte.	MacKintosh, John	2/12/15	
1438	Pte.	MacLean, Donald	25/9/15	
1111	Pte.	MacLean, Hugh Alexander	30/7/15	Wounded, 12/3/16.
1090	Pte.	MacLean, William	9/7/15	Died.
728	Pte.	MacRae, Edward	14/11/14	Killed, 13/5/15.
967	Pte.	Maggs, Cecil Herbert	4/2/15	Died..
1139	Pte.	Major, Sidney Francis	14/8/15	
1681	Pte.	Mallagh, John	8/11/16	
1492	Pte.	Mallett, Algernon Crause Bathurst	18/11/15	
1604	Pte.	Mallinson, James Edwards	19/4/16	
1285	Pte.	Mandy, Edward Charles	30/8/15	Accidentally killed, 3/4/16.
892	Pte.	Mann, James Robert	28/12/14	
1198	L/Cpl.	Manning, John William	27/8/15	
1173	Pte.	Mardon, William Thomas	21/8/15	Died.
1354	Pte.	Maree, Cornelius Gert	14/9/15	
1291	Pte.	Maree, Philip Peter	28/8/15	
866	Pte.	Markham, Thomas Duncan Moodie	15/12/14	Wounded, 12/3/16.
1022	Pte.	Markides, George Paul	4/1/15	
1085	Pte.	Marnie, Fleming	19/1/15	Wounded, 12/3/16.
1547	Pte.	Marnie, Frederick Evan	9/2/16	
1519	Pte.	Marshall, Harry	7/1/16	
1210	Pte.	Marshall, Hodgson Anderson	31/8/15	
1075	L/Cpl.	Marshall, John Thomas	16/1/15	Wounded, 30/5/16.
687	Cpl.	Martens, John Christian	19/11/14	
905	Pte.	Martin, Leslie Allen	15/12/14	Killed, 14/7/15.
1306	Pte.	Maspero, Percy Reginald	31/8/15	
1647	Pte.	Massie, James Anderson	5/8/16	Died.
1222	Cpl.	Masters, Henry William	31/8/15	
1080	Pte.	Mathieson, Francis	18/1/15	

Attested.

1275	Cpl.	Matthews, Percy	31/8/15	
1245	Sgt.	Maurer, David	8/9/15	
713	Pte.	Mawdsley, George Henry	9/11/14	
305	Pte.	Mawdsley, William Frederick	23/10/14	
810	Pte.	Mayne, Andrew	23/11/14	Died, 9/2/17.
1481	Pte.	McAllister, James	4/11/15	Died at sea, 27/2/17.
895	Pte.	McAllister, William	29/12/14	
1017	Pte.	McAllister, William	4/1/15	
1651	Pte.	McArthur, Daniel	12/8/16	Died.
1680	Pte.	McArthur, Donald	4/11/16	
1148	Pte.	McBeth, Douglas	17/8/15	
1529	Pte.	McCall, John	20/1/16	Wounded, 17/8/16.
1225	Pte.	McCandlish, Thomas	6/9/15	
696	Pte.	McCarthy, John Maitland	17/11/14	
1325	Pte.	McComb, Henry Herbert	2/9/15	
836	L/Cpl.	McDonald, John	28/11/14	Died.
746	Pte.	McEacharn, Charles Malcolm	21/11/14	Mentioned in dispatches, *Lon. Gaz.*, 2/8/18. Died.
503	Cpl.	McFarlane, James	28/10/14	
1343	Pte.	McGarry, Thomas	13/9/15	
606	Sgt.	McGlinn, Edward Thomas	3/11/14	Died.
825	Pte.	McGregor, Donald	26/11/14	
1630	Pte.	McGregor, George Alexander	14/6/16	
1654	Pte.	McGregor, John Peter Campbell	21/8/16	
1649	Pte.	McGregor, Peter Sleath	7/8/16	Killed, 24/11/17.
1263	Pte.	McIlwraith, Samuel	28/8/15	
1152	Pte.	McIver, Murdock	18/8/15	
1153	Sgt.	McIver, William Matheson	18/8/15	Died.
1650	Pte.	McKinlay, Walter	12/8/16	
1122	Pte.	McKinnon, Cowan Rankin	6/5/15	
1655	Pte.	McKnight, George	18/8/16	Died.
1675	Pte.	McLachlan, Albert Henry	26/10/16	Died, 13/4/17.
472	Pte.	McLaren, Charles William	27/10/14	
919	Pte.	McLean, Donald	29/12/14	
855	Pte.	McLean, James Smith	8/12/14	Killed, 11/3/16.
1685	Pte.	McLean, John Fraser	22/11/16	
941	Pte.	McLeod, James Matheson	9/1/15	
1477	Pte.	McMillan, Robert	20/10/15	
1684	Pte.	McNair, Robert	21/11/16	
1353	Pte.	McNamara, Ralph	14/9/15	

IN EAST AFRICA 121

			Attested.	
965	L/Cpl.	McPhail, Hugh	30/1/15	Died.
1241	Pte.	McRae, Donald	9/9/15	
1044	Pte.	McShea, John Joseph	6/1/15	
702	L/Cpl.	Mead, Albert Harry Walter	7/11/14	
544	Pte.	Meagher, Michael	27/10/14	
1636	Pte.	Meintzes, John	8/7/16	
1013	Pte.	Mellish, Ronald Arthur	4/1/15	Wounded, 12/3/16.
555	Sgt.	Mellor, Samuel	27/10/14	Killed, 11/3/16.
1402	Pte.	Melville, Henry	7/9/15	Wounded, 12/2/16.
1050	Pte.	Memory, John Adrian	11/1/15	
1671	Pte.	Menzies, William Peterson	14/10/16	Died.
1430	Pte.	Merchant, James	20/9/15	
199	Pte.	Meredith, Herbert James	20/10/14	
822	L/Cpl.	Metelerkamp, George	21/12/14	Died.
1008	Sgt.	Michie, M.B.E., Andrew	4/1/15	
1593	Pte.	Miles, Claude Picton	10/4/16	
957	Pte.	Miles, Griffith John	14/1/15	
1123	L/Cpl.	Miller, Ernest	7/8/15	
1303	Pte.	Miller, Percy William	27/8/15	
1440	Pte.	Milne, John	27/9/15	
758	Pte.	Mills, Claude	24/11/14	
1342	Pte.	Minnie, Frank John	3/9/15	
1400	Pte.	Miskin, Leonard Hulley	6/9/15	
1485	Pte.	Mitchell, George	4/11/15	
1539	Pte.	Mitchell, James Hamilton	1/2/16	Wounded, 12/3/16.
1448	Pte.	Moffatt, Alexander Jeffries	29/9/15	
1401	Pte.	Moller, Theodar	4/9/15	
1622	Pte.	Moneypenny, William Joseph	20/5/16	
1338	L/Cpl.	Montgomery, Samuel	26/8/15	
1015	Pte.	Moodie, Richard	5/1/15	Wounded, 12/3/16.
1193	Pte.	Moore, Robert Phillipps	26/8/15	Died, Salisbury, 28/6/17.
1515	Pte.	Moorhouse, William	6/1/16	Died, Voi, 14/3/16.
1512	Pte.	Morgan, Leonard Ray	3/1/16	
1161	Pte.	Morgan, Stanley Caleb	18/8/15	
1497	Pte.	Morgan, Thomas	27/11/15	
499	Pte.	Moroney, Patrick William	27/10/14	
498	L/Cpl.	Morris, David	27/10/14	Died, 28/7/16
1110	Pte.	Morrison, David Hugh Campbell	30/7/15	
630	Cpl.	Morrison, Robert Stark	6/11/14	Died of wounds, 16/3/16.
1244	Pte.	Mossop, Leslie John	10/9/15	
934	Pte.	Muller, John Frederick	7/1/15	

THE 2ND RHODESIA REGIMENT

			Attested.	
1314	Pte.	Munro, Emile Maxmillian	6/9/15	
1310	Pte.	Murison, George	31/8/15	
1227	Pte.	Murray, John William	8/9/15	Died, Salisbury, 13/9/17.
660	Pte.	Musgrave, Gerald Harry	10/9/16	Died.
900	Sgt.	Napper, Edward Robert	9/11/14	
1048	Pte.	Nash, Hassil Howard	11/1/15	Died.
1657	Pte.	Naylor, Fred.	31/8/16	
1505	Pte.	Needham, Francis Joseph Rowe	7/12/15	
1106	Pte.	Neezer, William John Worthington	28/7/15	
1264	Pte.	Nel, Thomas Johannes	26/8/15	
873	Pte.	Nelson, Lewis Joseph	18/12/14	
798	Pte.	Nelson, Walter Alfred	5/12/14	Killed, 8/5/15.
1404	Pte.	Nettleton, Bertram Atkinson	7/9/15	
1202	Pte.	Neville, John	28/8/15	
1162	Pte.	New, Douglas Seymour	19/8/15	
1602	Pte.	Newman, Richard George	18/4/16	
877	Pte.	Nicholl, Edgar	18/12/14	
1183	Pte.	Nicholls, Henry Perry	25/8/15	
1170	L/Cpl.	Nicholson, George Robert	20/8/15	
815	Pte.	Nicolle, Philip	24/11/14	
1243	Pte.	Nimmo, Harry	10/9/15	
828	Pte.	Nimmo, James Henry	27/11/14	
1004	Pte.	Niven, Donald McLean	2/1/15	Died.
1308	Pte.	Nolan, Michael	30/8/15	
625	Pte.	Oates, Ernest	5/11/14	
1315	Pte.	Oates, John Valentine	30/8/15	
1479	Pte.	O'Dea, Francis Joseph	4/11/15	
679	Pte.	Oliff, Mercyn Erle	17/11/14	
1652	Pte.	Oliver, Charles Arthur	19/8/16	
576	Pte.	Onions, Edward Gordon	31/10/14	
1653	Pte.	Oosthuizen, Albert Nicholas	18/8/16	
727	Pte.	Oosthuizen, Christopher Drayling	20/11/14	
1405	Pte.	Orme, Thomas Julian	11/9/15	

IN EAST AFRICA 123

			Attested.	
1594	Pte.	Osborne, Harvey Glasson	14/4/16	
1134	Pte.	O'Shea, Justin Gerald	16/8/15	
1406	Sgt.	Ott, Maximillian Carl	6/9/15	
998	Pte.	Packman, Harry	7/3/15	
1092	Cpl.	Palfrey, Willaim Les Charles	9/7/15	Wounded, 12/3/16.
1061	Pte.	Partridge, George Arthur	13/1/15	Killed, 11/3/16.
489	Pte.	Passmore, Cecil Neville	27/10/14	Died, 1/7/15.
901	Sgt.	Paterson, O.B.E., John	8/12/14	Wounded, 12/3/16.
1408	Pte.	Payne, George Herbert	7/9/15	
1575	Cpl.	Peacock, Kenneth Douglas	21/3/16	Died, Morogoro, 18/1/17.
1461	L/Cpl.	Penn, Cecil Rhodes	20/9/15	
1407	Pte.	Penn, Henry Stephen	6/9/15	
714	Pte.	Peters, Frederick Theodore	9/11/14	
1432	Cpl.	Peyton, Richard Chinney	20/9/15	Wounded, 12/3/16.
1610	Pte.	Phillips, Herbert Melville Dallow	29/4/16	
924	Pte.	Phillips, Norman	30/12/14	
846	Pte.	Phillis, George Trimmer	7/12/14	
1570	L/Cpl.	Pidcock, John Lonsdale	11/3/16	
869	Pte.	Piggett, Herbert Edward	16/12/14	
1444	Pte.	Pinney, William Samuel	28/9/15	
1489	Pte.	Pipkin, Frederick	17/11/15	Died.
1185	Sgt.	Pitcher, Walter Stephen	25/8/15	Died.
1077	Pte.	Place, Alan Whitley	16/1/15	
1141	Pte.	Pluck, Frederick	16/8/15	
953	Pte.	Pollock, Frederick	13/1/15	
695	L/Cpl.	Pollock, Samuel McWilliam	19/11/14	
1409	Cpl.	Porter, John McIntosh	6/9/15	Died.
1157	Pte.	Potgieter, Frederick Jacobus Johannes	18/8/15	Died.
1261	Cpl.	Potter, David Webb	18/8/15	
930	Pte.	Potts, Geoffrey Cecil	6/1/15	Killed, 8/5/15.
1204	Cpl.	Powrie, Alexander	30/8/15	Died.
1686	Pte.	Pretorius, Johannes Lodrigues	22/11/16	
1294	Cpl.	Price, Franklin Denistoun Rose	27/8/15	
1521	Pte.	Price, William Francis	10/1/16	

THE 2ND RHODESIA REGIMENT

Attested.

1010	Pte.	Puckle, Oswald	5/1/15	Killed, 12/2/16.
669	Pte.	Rainsford, Eric Anthony	14/11/14	
1540	Pte.	Ramsay, William Ramsay	3/2/16	
1166	Pte.	Reading, George Henry Rufus	20/8/15	
1037	Cpl.	Reckenzaun, Augustus	8/1/15	Died.
1435	Pte.	Reed, Benjamin	23/9/15	
672	Pte.	Reed, Thomas	14/11/14	
1247	Pte.	Reeder, Horace	27/8/15	
1265	Pte.	Reeks, Frederick George	31/8/15	
1456	Pte.	Rennie, John	7/10/15	
1234	Pte.	Renniker, Edward	8/9/15	Wounded, 17/8/16.
1221	Sgt.	Rettie, Henry James	4/9/15	
1533	Pte.	Reynolds, Alan Lowe	31/1/16	
1041	Pte.	Reynolds, James Thomas Harvey	9/1/15	Wounded, 11/3/16.
1531	Pte.	Rice, James	27/1/16	
1581	Pte.	Richards, Fred Woodford Glyn	30/3/16	Died, Handeni, 10/8/16.
980	L/Cpl.	Richards, William Harold	17/2/15	Wounded, 12/2/16.
609	L/Cpl.	Richardson, D.C.M., James Robert	4/11/14	Died.
1410	Pte.	Ritchie, Alfred	2/9/15	Wounded, 12/3/16.
1412	Pte.	Ritman, Joseph Edward	7/9/15	Wounded, 1/9/17.
1621	Pte.	Robbie, Andrew Crichton	20/5/16	
689	Sgt.	Roberts, Edward Pinkerton	19/11/14	
880	Pte.	Roberts, James William	21/12/14	
817	Pte.	Roberts, Shirley Walter	29/11/14	Died, Umtali, 29/5/17.
1357	Pte.	Robertson, Andrew Cornell	16/9/15	
769	R.S.M.	Robertson, George Leslie	26/11/14	Wounded, 13/5/15.
1277	Pte.	Robertson, Peter	31/8/15	
970	L/Cpl.	Robertson, William Brown	4/2/15	
1590	Pte.	Rodger, William	5/4/16	
1211	Pte.	Roets, Christian Peter	1/9/15	
1031	Pte.	Rogers, Albert Borrows	8/1/15	
1413	Pte.	Rollins, Henry	10/9/15	
558	Pte.	Roodt, Paul James	30/10/14	
1071	Pte.	Rose-Innes, Cosmo William Gordon Innes	15/1/15	
956	Pte.	Rosenbloom, David	19/1/15	
1206	C.S.M.	Ross, William Cargill	30/8/15	Died.
1451	Pte.	Rothstein, Louis	4/10/15	Wounded, 30/8/16.
1174	Pte.	Rounthwaite, Thomas	21/8/15	

IN EAST AFRICA 125

			Attested.	
1411	Pte.	Rourke, Joseph	8/9/15	Wounded, 12/3/16.
1483	Pte.	Rowan, William	13/11/15	
1288	Pte.	Rowe, Arthur Henry	6/9/15	
1555	Pte.	Rubenstein, Harry	16/2/16	
1493	Pte.	Rugg, Cecil William	19/11/15	
1437	Pte.	Rushton, Harold Evelyn	25/9/15	
496	Cpl.	Russell, George Innes	27/10/14	
1441	Pte.	Russell, Thomas Leopold	28/9/15	Died.
497	Sgt.	Rutherfoord, Arthur Henry	27/10/14	Died.
1305	Pte.	Sage, John Henry Creswell	31/8/15	
1184	Pte.	Salter, Hubert Alfred	25/8/15	
754	Pte.	Samuels, Rueben	23/11/14	
1099	Pte.	Saunders, John Thomas Hollingshead	16/7/15	
422	Pte.	Saunders, Percival Goldring	24/10/14	
645	Pte.	Savage, George	9/11/14	
969	Sgt.	Savory, Thomas Robert Landy	4/2/15	Died, Salisbury, 1/10/17.
699	Cpl.	Sayer, Charles John	20/11/14	
1687	Pte.	Sayer, Walter Ernest	26/11/16	
1064	Pte.	Schunck, George Bryan	14/1/15	Killed, 11/3/16.
1464	Pte.	Scollard, Nicholas	19/9/15	
1618	Pte.	Scott, Alexander McLaren	13/5/16	
1068	Sgt.	Scott, Edgar	15/1/15	
844	Sgt.	Scott, George	5/12/14	
703	Pte.	Scott, William Allen	7/11/14	
788	Pte.	Scott, William Taylor	1/12/14	Died.
1266	Pte.	Seagrief, John James	3/9/15	
806	Pte.	Seward, Harry	21/11/14	Killed, 11/3/16.
1281	Pte.	Seward, Richard Ambrose	27/8/15	Killed, 17/8/16.
1453	Pte.	Seymour, John Edward	4/10/15	
1552	Pte.	Shakeshaft, John Montague	13/2/16	Died.
1189	Pte.	Shanahan, Michael Francis	26/8/15	
1557	Pte.	Sharp, John Frost	16/2/16	
1415	Pte.	Sharp, John Healey	7/9/15	
670	Sgt.	Sharpe, Donald	14/11/14	
1267	Pte.	Shaw, M.M., Arnold Bramwell	6/9/15	Awarded M.M., *Lon. Gaz.*, 12/4/17. Mentioned in dispatches, 8/2/17.
827	Cpl.	Shaw, Thomas	26/11 14	

			Attested.	
520	Pte.	Sheard, Cecil	29/10/14	
1095	Pte.	Shelton, Thomas William Lindsay	14/7/15	
1541	Pte.	Shepherd, Thomas Herbert	4/2/16	
1476	Pte.	Shields, John Ross	26/10/15	
1188	Pte.	Sievwright, George Strachan	25/8/15	
801	Pte.	Simmonds, Frederick	19/11/14	
1414	Pte.	Simpson, Robert	9/9/15	
1035	Pte.	Singer, Walter Douglas	8/1/15	
1491	Pte.	Slabbert, Matas Johannes	17/11/15	Died.
1059	Pte.	Sleggs, Fred Henry	12/1/15	
1256	Pte.	Slement, John	27/8/15	
1522	Pte.	Smart, Arthur Leopold	10/1/16	Wounded, 12/3/16.
646	Pte.	Smedley, Dallas Dermot	9/11/14	
1416	Pte.	Smit, Lawrence	6/9/15	Died.
1673	Pte.	Smith Charles	15/10/16	
972	L/Cpl.	Smith, Charles Herbert	9/2/15	Wounded, 12/3/16.
1168	L/Cpl.	Smith, Edmund William Russell	20/8/15	
922	Pte.	Smith, Edward Charles	30/12/14	
1418	Pte.	Smith, Edward Charles Percival	11/9/15	Wounded, 11/3/16.
950	L/Sgt.	Smith, Fergus Jardine Menzies	13/1/15	
1670	Pte.	Smith, Gerald Pemberton	12/10/16	
1417	Pte.	Smith, Samuel Jacob	27/8/15	
1109	Pte.	Smith, Stewart	28/7/15	
1164	Pte.	Smith, Sydney Harold	20/8/15	
615	Col/Sgt.	Smith, William Dundas	4/11/14	
1003	Pte.	Smith, William Dudley Ward	30/12/14	
608	Pte.	Southey, Ivor Henry	4/11/14	
701	Pte.	Speck, Walter	7/11/14	
655	L/Cpl.	Spencer, Wallace Keedwell	11/11/14	Died, 12/6/16.
500	Pte.	Springer, Harry	27/10/14	
1000	Pte.	Standage, James	30/12/14	
1042	L/Cpl.	Standen, Arthur Edward	7/1/15	
1585	Pte.	Standish, John Selwyn	2/4/16	
1329	Pte.	Stanley, Aubrey Mervyn	31/8/15	
1633	Pte.	Stedman, Frederick Smallman	24/6/16	
1486	Pte.	Stenhouse, Alexander Mitchell	13/11/15	Died.

IN EAST AFRICA 127

			Attested.	
993	L/Cpl.	Stephen, Alan James	5/3/15	Wounded, 11/3/16. Died.
1326	Pte.	Stephens, Alexander Herbert	30/8/15	
1076	Pte.	Stevens, Frank	16/1/15	
544	Pte.	Stevens, George Frederick Fountain	29/10/14	
1323	L/Cpl.	Stewart, Robert Thomas Bealby	30/8/15	
805	C.Q.M.S.	Stidolph, Neville Harold	21/11/14	Wounded, 12/3/16.
1631	Pte.	Stodart, William Swan	21/6/16	
1125	Pte.	Stols, Gabriel Joseph	7/8/15	
1436	Pte.	Stone, Harold Alfred	29/5/15	
1588	Pte.	Stow, William Philipson	2/4/16	
814	Cpl.	Stratton, Henry Scott	24/11/14	Wounded, 12/2/16.
878	Pte.	Strobel, Victor Frank	18/12/14	
1545	Pte.	Struthers, Archibald	7/2/16	
1175	Pte.	Struthers, John Watson Jack	21/8/15	
1600	Pte.	Stuart, Charles Travers	16/4/16	Died, Dar-es-Salaam, 2/2/17.
1192	Pte.	Susman, Oscar	28/8/15	Died.
1129	Pte.	Susman, William Myer	10/8/15	
826	Pte.	Sutherland, John	26/11/14	Died, 14/9/15.
1466	Pte.	Swann, William Nyls St. Augustine	11/10/15	
1214	Pte.	Swartz, Daniel Andries	1/9/15	
1149	Pte.	Swartz, Gideon John	18/8/15	
770	Pte.	Swartz, John	27/11/14	
910	Pte.	Sybray, James Blackwell	17/12/14	
898	Pte.	Symington, Ernest	30/12/14	
1443	Pte.	Symons, Henry Thomas	27/9/15	
1339	Pte.	Tait, Murdoch Morrison	31/8/15	
989	Pte.	Tapson, Walter Noel	1/3/15	
1523	Pte.	Tarr, Owen James	12/1/16	
807	Sgt.	Tatnell, Percy	21/11/14	
1065	Pte.	Taylor, Charles Oliver	14/1/15	
438	Pte.	Taylor, Hugh Glyn	26/10/14	Died, 6/8/16.
1420	Pte.	Taylor, John	6/9/15	
1496	Pte.	Taylor, Joseph Collins	21/11/15	Died of wounds, 11/7/16.
1603	Pte.	Tebbutt, Ernest	18/4/16	
1538	Pte.	Temple, William Joseph	1/2/15	Died.
837	Pte.	Theal, Charles William Auchtal	1/12/14	
1240	Pte.	Thomas, Arthur	9/9/15	
932	Pte.	Thomas, John Dudley	7/1/15	

THE 2ND RHODESIA REGIMENT

			Attested.	
736	L/Cpl.	Thompson, Aubrey Victor	18/11/14	
1568	Pte.	Thompson, Joseph Harold Penwick	4/3/16	
1131	Pte.	Thompson, Richard	10/8/15	Died.
871	Sgt.	Thompson, M.M., William	16/12/14	Awarded M.M., *Lon. Gaz.*, 14/12/17.
1569	Pte.	Thorne, Charles Henry	7/3/16	
856	L/Cpl.	Thorne, Stanley George	9/12/14	
550	Cpl.	Thorpe, Alan Octavius	29/10/14	
586	Pte.	Thorpe, Edgar Richard	2/11/14	
1028	Pte.	Thoss, Louis William	8/1/15	
748	Pte.	Thurtell, Charles	23/11/14	
1128	Pte.	Thurtell, Walter Henry	7/8/15	Died.
1215	Pte.	Tilbury, Henry James	1/9/15	
834	Pte.	Titley, William Addison	30/11/14	
1605	Pte.	Towns, James Hunter	19/4/16	Died, Bulawayo 19/5/17.
939	Pte.	Townsend, Albert Charles	13/1/15	
951	Pte.	Townsend, Charles Southgate	13/1/15	Killed, 8/5/15.
407	Cpl.	Trapp, Frank Renney	24/10/14	
1287	Pte.	Trappler, Harry Leopold	21/8/15	
1316	Pte.	Trappler, Maurice	31/8/15	
1268	Pte.	Treunick, Daniel Johannes	1/9/15	
1572	Pte.	Trollip, Donovan Spencer Hannibel	15/3/16	
1002	Pte.	Trott, M.M., Arthur Sholto	2/1/15	Mentioned in dispatches, *Lon. Gaz.*, 8/2/17. Awarded M.M., *Lon. Gaz.*, 12 3/17. Died, Maitland, 19/2/17.
842	Pte.	Tulloch, Ian	5/12/14	
1449	Pte.	Tully, Mynett Boyd	29/9/15	Died.
793	Sgt.	Turner, Frederick George	5/12/14	Died, 17/5/16.
1419	Pte.	Turner, John Butler	7/9/15	
716	Sgt.	Turner, Morrison	9/11/14	
1104	Pte.	Tyler, Seth Frederick	26/7/15	
1345	Pte.	Tyrrell, Timothy Harold	13/9/15	Died.
1421	Pte.	Underwood, George	8/9/15	
661	Pte.	Underwood, Lewis	12/11/14	
1422	Pte.	Urquhart, Andreis	8/9/15	

IN EAST AFRICA   129

			Attested.	
1276	Pte.	Uys, Mathays Michael	3/9/15	
1040	Pte.	Uys, William Petrus Meyer	8/1/15	
779	Pte.	Valancy, Richard	30/11/14	
1556	Pte.	Van Blerk, Matthew	16/2/16	
1269	Pte.	Van der Merwe, John Jacobus	3/9/15	
783	Pte.	Van der Spuy, Sybrand Jacobus	30/11/14	
1558	Pte.	Van der Venter, William Adrian	17/2/16	
675	Pte.	Van der Walt, Frederick	16/11/14	
1598	Pte.	Van der Walt, Gert	15/4/16	Died, 8/9/16.
1133	Pte.	Van Eetveld, John Frank Peter	13/8/15	
1038	Pte.	Van Eetveld, John Wesley	8/1/15	
1677	Pte.	Van Heerden, Gerriat	1/11/16	
1423	Pte.	Van Heerden, Henry	7/9/15	Wounded, 12/2/16.
1678	Pte.	Van Heerden, Jacob Lewis	3/11/16	
1544	Pte.	Van Niekerk, Benjamin	5/2/16	Died.
648	Pte.	Van Niekerk, Nicholas Jacobus	10/11/14	
1160	Pte.	Van Rooyen, Jeremiah Joseph	18/8/15	
1021	L/Cpl.	Van Schalkwyk, Henning, Jacobus	5/1/15	
1322	Pte.	Van Wyk, Andries Petrus	3/9/15	
1628	Pte.	Vennings, Herman	7/6/16	
1073	L/Sgt.	Vernon, Dayrell Tassie	16/1/15	
863	Pte.	Vernon, Evelyn Harcourt	14/12/14	Killed, 5/6/15.
1143	L/Cpl.	Vernon, Robert Cecil	16/8/15	Died.
1452	Pte.	Vickers, Richard	4/10/15	
1549	Pte.	Viljeon, Martin Philip	9/2/16	
1620	Pte.	Viljeon, Richard Henry	20/5/16	
906	Pte.	Vincent, John	15/12/14	
1270	Pte.	Viviers, William Johannes	6/9/15	
1537	Pte.	Von Broembsen, Robert Herman	1/2/16	Wounded, 12/3/16.
1074	Pte.	Voslee, Jurney Wessels	16/1/15	
1271	Pte.	Waites, Harold Davies Levy	6/9/15	
1066	Pte.	Walker, Alec John	7/1/15	
1567	Pte.	Walker, Innes Cameron	5/3/16	

			Attested.	
1426	Pte.	Wallace, Harold	6/9/15	
1346	Pte.	Waller, Robert Harold Eustace	13/9/15	
985	Pte.	Walmisley, Revel Featherstone	23/2/15	
809	Pte.	Walsh, Herman Cellier	23/11/14	
1535	Pte.	Walshe, Edward Varian	31/1/16	
1536	Pte.	Walter, George	20/1/16	
1272	Pte.	Walton, Charles Lawrence		
511	L/Cpl.	Walton, Cyril Guy Montague	28/10/14	
1057	Pte.	Ward, William Denny	11/1/15	Died.
890	Pte.	Warner, Carl Henry	24/12/14	
1425	Pte.	Warren, Robert	6/9/15	
861	Pte.	Warren, Wilfried Ernest	12/12/14	
1107	Pte.	Waters, Thomas William	28/7/15	
1115	Pte.	Watkins, Frederick Daniels	28/7/15	
1176	Pte.	Watkins, Horace Lloyd	21/8/15	
851	Cpl.	Watkins, Jesse Thomas	8/12/14	
1532	Pte.	Watson, Alfred Tyndale	27/1/16	Wounded, 12/3/16.
891	Pte.	Watson, Henry Frank	28/12/14	Died.
1465	Pte.	Watson, John	19/9/15	
1471	Pte.	Watts, Willie	16/10/15	
1179	L/Cpl.	Weale, Philip Ingham	23/8/15	
552	Pte.	Webb, Frank	29/10/14	
1573	Pte.	Weedon, Ernest Kynaston	14/3/16	
1551	Pte.	Welch, Lawrence	12/2/16	
991	Pte.	Welensky, D.C.M., Benjamin Michael	2/3/15	
704	Cpl.	Wells, Ernest Morris	7/11/14	Killed, 8/5/15.
502	Sgt.	Wells, Owen Thomas	27/10/14	
1167	Pte.	Welsh, Thomas Clayton	25/8/15	
1283	Cpl.	Wessels, Christian	31/8/15	
843	Pte.	West, Daniel	5 12/14	
1239	Pte.	Whales, Alfred	9/9/15	
1012	Pte.	Wheatley, Leslie Warner	2/1/15	
421	Pte.	White, Granville Marcus	24/10/14	Killed, 17/8/16.
654	Pte.	White, Harry Frank	11/11/14	
749	Pte.	White, James Charles	23/11/14	
1530	Pte.	White, John	27/1/16	
440	Pte.	White, John Neville	26/10/14	
886	Pte.	White, Thomas Otho Shearburne	24/12/14	

IN EAST AFRICA

Attested.

No.	Rank	Name	Attested	Notes
889	Pte.	Whitehead, Richard	26/12/14	Died, 30/7/17.
1524	Pte.	Whitfield, Robert Lee Havelock	16/1/16	
975	Pte.	Whitmore, Frank Charles	15/2/15	
1428	Pte.	Whyte, Colin Campbell	18/9/15	
593	Pte.	Wicks, Arthur Robert	2/11/14	
1473	Pte.	Wilkins, M.M., William Turner	17/10/15	Wounded, 12/3/16
1668	Pte.	Wilkinson, Henry Frederick	6/10/16	
1356	Pte.	Will, Gordon Davidson	15/9/15	
1546	Pte.	Williams, Alfred	7/2/16	
439	Pte.	Williams, David Arnold	26/10/14	
857	Pte.	Williams, Edward Owen	12/12/14	
1258	Pte.	Williams, Griffin Lloyd	31/8/15	
796	Pte.	Williams, John Howard	5/12/14	Died.
992	Pte.	Williams, Leopold	5/3/15	
471	Pte.	Williamson, Hugh	27/10/14	
759	Pte.	Wilson, Alexander Dalrymple Oliver	24/11/14	
960	Pte.	Wilson, Benjamin John	21/1/15	
1509	Pte.	Wilson, Charles William	14/12/15	
591	Pte.	Wilson, Edwin	2/11/14	
668	Pte.	Wilson, John Henry	14/11/14	Died, 11/8/16
1348	Pte.	Wilson, Ronald Selby Champion	14/9/15	Died, 13/3/17.
1424	Pte.	Wilson, Thomas	9/9/15	
674	Pte.	Wilson, William George	16/11/14	
1118	Pte.	Winter, Hugh Stanley	31/7/15	Wounded, 17/8/16. Died.
664	Pte.	Withams, James Henry	13/11/14	
865	Sgt.	Wolters, Nicholas Charles	12/12/14	
685	Sgt.	Wood, Clement George	18/11/14	Wounded, 30/5/16.
1146	Pte.	Wood, Harold William	17/8/15	
923	Pte.	Woodend, Frank Poole	30/12/14	
1562	Pte.	Woodhouse, Alfred Henry	1/3/16	
1503	Pte.	Woods, Charles	23/11/15	Wounded, 12/3/16.
1097	Pte.	Woods, Ernest Frederick	19/7/15	
617	Sgt.	Woods, Sydney (was Graham)	4/11/14	

			Attested.	
1514	Pte.	Woolacott, Nathaniel	5/1/16	
940	Pte.	Wordsworth, Arthur Lawrence	9/1/15	
1632	Pte.	Wright, Raleigh Mitford Shawe	31/6/16	Died.
719	Pte.	Yeatman, Edward	10/11/14	Died.
757	Pte.	Younghusband Samuel Thorpe	24/11/14	Wounded, 6/8/16.
925	Pte.	Yuille, Andrew	30/12/14